Michael Hastings was born in 1938 and lived in South London for seventeen years. At fifteen he commenced a three-year apprenticeship in bespoke tailoring. He has written five novels – *The Game* (1957), *The Frauds* (1959), *Tussy is Me* (1968), *The Nightcomers* (1971) and *And in the Forest the Indians* (1975); a collection of short stories, *Bart's Mornings and Other Tales of Modern Brazil* (1975); and two biographies, *Rupert Brooke: 'The Handsomest Young Man in England'* (1969) and *Sir Richard Burton* (1978).

His plays are: *Don't Destroy Me*, directed by Robert Peake, 1956; *Yes and After*, directed by John Dexter, 1957; *The World's Baby*, directed by Patrick Dromgoole, 1964; *For the West (Congo)*, directed by Toby Robertson, 1965; *Blue as His Eyes the Tin Helmet He Wore*, directed by David Cunliffe, 1966; *Lee Harvey Oswald: 'a far mean streak of indepence brought on by negleck'*, directed by Peter Coe, 1967; *The Silence of Saint-Just*, directed by Walter Eyselink, 1972; *The Cutting of the Cloth*, unperformed autobiographic play, 1973; *For the West (Uganda)*, directed by Nicholas Wright, 1977; *Gloo Joo*, directed by Michael Rudman, 1978; *Full Frontal*, directed by Rufus Collins, 1979; *Carnival War a Go Hot*, directed by Antonia Bird, 1979; *Gloo Joo*, TV, directed by John Kaye Cooper, 1979; *Murder Rap*, directed by Peter Duffell, 1980, and *Midnight at the Starlight* directed by John Glenister, 1980.

Michael Hastings has won several awards, including the Academy of Arts and Sciences 'Emmy', the Somerset Maugham Award, the *Evening Standard* Comedy of the Year, BAFTA and Writers' Guild awards.

Three Plays

Gloo Joo
Full Frontal
For the West (Uganda)

MICHAEL HASTINGS

Penguin Books

Penguin Books Ltd, Harmondsworth, Middlesex, England
Penguin Books, 625 Madison Avenue, New York, New York 10022, U.S.A.
Penguin Books Australia Ltd, Ringwood, Victoria, Australia
Penguin Books Canada Ltd, 2801 John Street, Markham, Ontario, Canada L3R 1B4
Penguin Books (N.Z.) Ltd, 182–190 Wairau Road, Auckland 10, New Zealand

—

Published in Penguin Books 1980

Gloo Joo copyright © Michael Hastings, 1980
Full Frontal copyright © Michael Hastings, 1980
For the West (*Uganda*) copyright © Michael Hastings, 1980
All rights reserved

Set, printed and bound in Great Britain by
Cox & Wyman Ltd, Reading
Set in Monotype Times

CONTENTS

For Victoria

Gloo Joo

Gloo Joo was first presented at the Hampstead Theatre, London, on 20 September 1978; and at the Criterion Theatre, Piccadilly, on 9 November 1978, with the following cast:

Meadowlark Rachel Warner	OSCAR JAMES
Irene Connor	HEATHER TOBIAS
Raymond Borrall	ANTONY BROWN
Gerry Radinski	DAVE HILL
Elliott Brucknell	EDWARD HALSTED
Edna Walter	AKOSUA BUSIA

Directed by Michael Rudman
Designed by Poppy Mitchell

CHARACTERS

MEADOWLARK RACHEL WARNER, British/Jamaican in his early thirties

IRENE CONNOR, lovely woman, with a rough edge to her, slightly tired, in her late twenties, a faint accent in her voice

RAYMOND BORRALL, thin and fastidious and in his late forties

GERRY RADINSKI, broad explosive nature, humour and passion and thickness, around forty

ELLIOTT BRUCKNELL, ascetic lugubrious man, perhaps younger than he looks

EDNA WALTER, early twenties, very much in bloom and disconcertingly to the point, black Guyana born

ACT ONE

Market end of Coldharbour Lane, Brixton, 1978.
> [*The centre of the stage behind the glass panels is* MEADOW-
> LARK'*s room. The lights come up.* RAYMOND *starts ham-
> mering on the door to* MEADOWLARK'*s room.*
> RAYMOND *hammering . . .*]

RAYMOND: Mr Meadowlark Rachel Warner? Mr Meadowlark
Rachel Warner?

MEADOWLARK'S VOICE: Who de ras?

RAYMOND: Mr Warner?

MEADOWLARK'S VOICE: If et's de bill from the Jamaican
patti shop, it ent fer I, is fer teh guy was here before
a here, an I is en here anyhow, so slip it unner teh door
ta.

RAYMOND: Mr M. R. Warner? 397 Coldharbour Lane, SW9,
first floor, room thirteen?

MEADOWLARK'S VOICE: Ef it's teh congratulate meh on meh
grett dey or I winnin the Kingston Brown Sugar Rum Raffle
lars year, slip et unner teh door, ta.

RAYMOND: *Mr Warner* will you please open the door.

MEADOWLARK: You is the police man.

RAYMOND: No, sir. Will you please open the door. I am not the
police.
> [*Hidden from view the door unlocks. A violent scuffle. A loud
> shout from* IRENE.]

MEADOWLARK'S VOICE: What is yerh den, mon?

GERRY: Right! Got him!

RAYMOND: Down the stairs! That's right, sir!

MEADOWLARK: De ras!
> [RAYMOND *appears through the front door stage right.*
> MEADOWLARK *follows held by* GERRY.]

RAYMOND: If you'll just step outside with us, sir.

MEADOWLARK: Who de hell is yeh, mon? Am skin nekked.

RAYMOND: I am an immigration officer attached to the Office of Appeals, Immigration Centre, Gatwick.

MEADOWLARK: Teh rars yer is.

RAYMOND: I am empowered by the Home Office as of April 10 last to restrain you for removal to my office under the directions of a warrant in my possession. Are you Meadowlark Rachel Warner?

MEADOWLARK: I not positive is I at all at all, you know now, dis ting could become a big diplomatic cause of confusion. This warrant for meh arrest?

RAYMOND: No. It is an order to restrain you for removal to my office under the Immigration Act '71.

MEADOWLARK: Some confusion buildin up in meh mind between restraint and arrest.

[IRENE *follows on behind down the steps. She wears a bra and pants and tries to pull on her dress.*]

IRENE: Meadowlark! What you done then?

[*As* MEADOWLARK *turns and struggles in* GERRY's *firm armlock.*]

MEADOWLARK: Swear to Goh I don't know, ras! You hurtin Blue Nose!

GERRY: It's all right Ray, I got him tight.

MEADOWLARK: No shit mon Ray he got me tight.

[*It is a complicated armlock.* IRENE *pulls at* GERRY's *arm.* RAYMOND *holds her away.*]

IRENE: Sod off him then!

[*As* MEADOWLARK *struggles* GERRY *produces a pair of handcuffs and eventually snaps them down on* MEADOWLARK's *wrists against the floor.*]

GERRY: That's it, boy! . . . There you go!

[*He hauls* MEADOWLARK *back to his feet.*]

Just in case you want to catch me unawares. Got a knife have you?

MEADOWLARK: Get off! En enerested en your underwares in teh least.

GERRY: By the powers invested in me I am authorized to restrain you on the grounds you wilfully avoided this officer here in the pursuance of his duty.

RAYMOND: Sorry son, but Mr Radinski here is new to my department.

GERRY [*reading warrant*]: Section 8, paragraph 14 'forcible restraint on removal on objection to foreigner's desire to avoid dutiful destination'.

MEADOWLARK: Hey mon. Yer born talkin lekk tis?

IRENE: What he done for Christ's sake!

RAYMOND [*to* MEADOWLARK]: My records show, Mr Warner, you were advised three times to appeal against this order a year ago. Records show you have expressly disregarded the offices of the Immigration Appeal Court, and also the Appeal Tribunal, and finally the government-appointed Adjudicator. Records show all legal process has been exhausted and it is my job to take you to the office at Gatwick and sign you out.

MEADOWLARK: Is yer serious? Out where yer outin me?

GERRY: Mr Borrall is an officer empowered to provide aliens with removal to place of deportation under the terms of Notice of Removal Instructions, son.

[MEADOWLARK *still seems very confused. He stares.*]

MEADOWLARK: Where meh rassin trousers Irene?

IRENE: They want to throw you out the country. Meadowlark, do something!

MEADOWLARK: Outa what?

RAYMOND: Do you possess a certificate of patriality in your room upstairs?

[MEADOWLARK'S *confusion.*]

IRENE [*to* MEADOWLARK]: Papers, documents . . . !

MEADOWLARK: No mon, possess nuttin.

RAYMOND: Possess a passport of any sort?

MEADOWLARK: No, mon.

RAYMOND: Possess any form of identity, work permit –

MEADOWLARK: No mon got no identity no. Is I Meadowlark.

GERRY: Are you prepared to come peaceably and voluntarily?

MEADOWLARK: An is was goin teh be ter grettest day of meh liffe, yer know.

IRENE: Oh come off it! You bastards ain't taking him off without his clothes! Ay!

MEADOWLARK: Am in cryin need of meh trousers, Irene.

IRENE: I'll get them.

MEADOWLARK [*as she goes back up the stairs*]: An meh tone shirt an teh yellow size nines fer meh aching cold feet yer know.

IRENE [*hurrying*]: OK!

GERRY: And who is Irene?

MEADOWLARK: I see yer lookin, big eyes. Irene jus a frien step by say she wants to tekk me to Catford tonight for ter dog-trackin cos she bought the tickets an all lekk a good gerl not knowing whether a got money or not.

GERRY: I see. Someone you live off, ay?

MEADOWLARK: I having this suspicion lars night, there was no sun all day, and ten teh moon don't shine, an yer two blue meanies on meh doorstep at half-past six in teh mornin.

GERRY: So?

MEADOWLARK: Mer ole man used teh say he said, 'Tell yer tit straight, boy, if de sun don't come up in de day, and teh moon en in no great hurries come out in night time, duck yer head beneath the sheets, mon, cos it de end ob de fokkin worl . . .'

[IRENE *comes back with jacket and trousers and shoes and shirt.*]

GERRY: So?

MEADOWLARK: Then a meet with yer two shits don't I? Meh daddy was right.

[IRENE *helps* MEADOWLARK *into his trousers. She pulls his shoes on for him.*]

IRENE: Fuck's sake Meadowlark think of something!

MEADOWLARK: Am tinking fast, mon, shit!

IRENE: Well, think!

MEADOWLARK: Don't rush et, teh thinkin's cetchin meh up now.

IRENE [*to* GERRY]: The cuffs, copper?!

GERRY: He goes without the shirt then.

[*She pushes the shirt and jacket over* MEADOWLARK's *shoulders. She stuffs the shirt-tails in as best.*]

MEADOWLARK [*to* RAYMOND]: What was it sir, mon, yer got tat warrant for?

RAYMOND: It is a Deportation Order, Mr Warner.

MEADOWLARK: Yer carnt do this ter I.

RAYMOND: I'm afraid I can.

MEADOWLARK: I'm Bridish thru an thru. Besides this is teh grettest day ob meh liffe, kindating.

RAYMOND: I'm very sorry about that but –

MEADOWLARK: Today – today's terh day I wed.

RAYMOND: Wed?

MEADOWLARK: Sure! . . . Sure! . . . Is today, mon!

RAYMOND: Today is Sunday.

IRENE: Wed? To *who*?

MEADOWLARK [*desperate*]: To yer darlin what you tink all I bin saying bout teh grettest day an all kindating?

IRENE: Meadowlark – that's the first I've heard of it?

MEADOWLARK: It was meant to be a big secret lekk. Yer weren't goin to know till the last momen ting.

IRENE: But –

MEADOWLARK: I done all tings right. De banns on teh church. De day in the church book. The priest spoke on teh phone wive me. An he all fixed up for this afternoon. Sudden what come along who should show up but tese two blue nose honkies full of crap! I telling the bible trute, mon.

IRENE: Married!

MEADOWLARK: I swear it Irene!

IRENE: Oh Meadowlark . . .

MEADOWLARK: Was matter? Yer en married already is yer after all?

IRENE [*thoughtfully*]: Meadowlark . . . Prove it!

MEADOWLARK: Teh ring girl, put yer han in meh pocket tere –

[*As* GERRY *makes a move for his pocket nervously.*]

Not you, mon, you got somethin all confused yer keeps yer

government restraint ting on yer sexual abdabs kindating!

[IRENE *pulls out a gold ring from his pocket. She puts it on her finger in amazement.*]

IRENE: It fits.

MEADOWLARK: I en no chump.

IRENE: Where'd you steal it?

MEADOWLARK: I been bought it . . . yeh believe me?

IRENE: No.

MEADOWLARK: Yeh gotta say yeh lovin me just a bit you know. - An all this goin on, too.

IRENE: Just . . . a little bit.

RAYMOND: Now Gerry.

[RAYMOND *and* GERRY *pull* MEADOWLARK *away.*]

IRENE: . . . You can't take him like that you bastards! I don't know where you're taking him to! You've got to tell me where? What about his clothes? What about me? You can't take him like a bleeding animal. He's got rights! I ain't letting you go like this! . . .

[*She follows.*]

Immigration Offices at Gatwick.

[*Larger space is walled with plain screens. Tic-tac furniture. Smaller space is* RAYMOND's *office. And telephone. The third space is behind the waiting-room glass panels stage left. As the lights come up* RAYMOND, GERRY *and* MEADOWLARK *are seated in the glass-panelled centre section.*]

RAYMOND: . . . Date of birth please? And . . . place of birth?

MEADOWLARK [*to* GERRY]: Yeh really change the colour of my skin round my wrists yeh have with dem bracelets.

GERRY: Shut your mouth and answer the questions!

MEADOWLARK: Is you bad on yeh natomy!

RAYMOND: Mr Warner. Your birth date?

MEADOWLARK: Yeh puttin down between July and August 1946 and yeh breathin fire close.

RAYMOND [*writing*]: Place of birth?

MEADOWLARK: SS *Corregidor*.

RAYMOND: Born on board ship bound for where?

MEADOWLARK: For famous England dummy! My daddy said I was born on ship Kingston/Southampton, an some kind of double trouble blew up because my mother is refused entry someting dodgy bout she entry permit and she say she want a divorce on the dock like that. And daddy jumpin and screamin left holdin me teh chile an mother took off back to Jamaica same boat, kind of ting.

RAYMOND: What did the Port Authorities accept for your father's legitimate claim for parenthood?

MEADOWLARK: Is you asking me? I was ten inches long and half of me stuck in a twist in his inside coat pocket and he havin a divorce on the Southampton dockside, I'm tellin, I'm lucky he never toss me over side of the dock an feed me to teh gulls you know.

RAYMOND: What papers did the ship's captain sign for your birth certificate?

MEADOWLARK: Yeh serious? My daddy never believed I was his like, and I was born at the bottom of the boat in out of the way cabin you know. My mummy said it all en shameful, an he just want excuse to send her back on home, man. He thinking he find his new hot totty in Brixton, back den Brixton en all bad like it become now.

RAYMOND: Your father is a legalized immigrant *circa* 1946?

MEADOWLARK: He legal no mistake, no mistakin my daddy sir, he been legally dead now for eight years. You get no more legal dan dat now?

RAYMOND: Schools attended? And last school you left before taking up initial employment?

MEADOWLARK: Daddy he not quite stay long enough any one place find a good school, an all, went to dis went to dat, fight here, fight dere, an I learn to read and write, man, an daddy say so long as can read and write the horse's name en de bookie's ticket, education nuff he say.

RAYMOND: Left school at fifteen?

MEADOWLARK: Leavin school all de time you know.

RAYMOND: First job?

MEADOWLARK: No deh first job never come along ligit I.

RAYMOND: Social Security number?

MEADOWLARK: A don't tink me an teh government ever got together on dat one.

RAYMOND: Last recorded place of employment and name of employer?

MEADOWLARK: Am thinkin yeh won't want them now, sir, I'm believing tey all doin time inside the famous Liverpool General Prison.

RAYMOND: And you do not possess a passport. Never been abroad.

MEADOWLARK: I bin abroad, man.

RAYMOND. I don't understand. How can you have been abroad if you possess no valid identity?

MEADOWLARK: I'm no ignorant black boy yeh got here. I bin back to Jamaica four times. Bin twice to France. An bin package trip wit my girl to Amsterdam. I use my daddy's passport after he dead. Put a dab of white on teh hair and grow a beard like this. S'far as white customs men yeh know all black bastards look like any other black bastards kindating.

RAYMOND: We'll disregard all the areas of general law infringement. You are one Meadowlark Rachel Warner. Born at sea approximately August 1946, last known address 397 Coldharbour Lane, London SW9. Last gainful means of employment unrecorded. And you do not possess any recognizably legal certificate of patriality. Nor any evidence that you or your parents resided in this country before 1962. All correct?

MEADOWLARK: Am tinkin it got teh ring of truth.

GERRY: Don't be facetious. Mr Borrall's about to read you the riot act, sonny.

RAYMOND: My colleague here is Mr Gerald Radinski. Gerry is seconded to me from the Port of London Aliens' Division. And I am Raymond Borrall. First Officer, Immigration Appeals Office, Gatwick. As a rule this building is a kind of final destination for any alien found in the country who has beyond all the bounds of appeal judication become an undesirable resident. And for whom there is no further legal resource. For whom it is my duty to carry out an order in deportation – in your case – in pursuance of the Commonwealth Immigrants Act 1971, Section 2, para 9.

MEADOWLARK: What a done wrong den?

RAYMOND: According to your file, you were given at least three opportunities to present yourself to an appeal tribunal to prove lawful and rightful stay in this country. You ignored all notices to prove your case to the Home Office.

MEADOWLARK: I having this notion havin bin inside dem youth detention camps, an havin been in the Isle of Wight Prison, if a see a summons creepycrawly in de door mat, am reachin for my woolly top, brother, an am leavin out teh window.

RAYMOND [*from the file*]: Furthermore, the UK Immigrants Advisory Service made repeated representations to the tribunal for stay of execution of my order until you could declare.

MEADOWLARK: Nothin to declare yeh know, am just Meadowlark that all, en got nothin but a sack full of woolly tops.

GERRY: Declare for your own defence, bonehead, he mean.

MEADOWLARK: Am got no defence, a en tellin yeh more now case yeh cut I golden balls off.

RAYMOND: I am hereby enforced to state that there remains no legal channel left open to you. Nor is there any appeal left open to you on objection to removal to your destination.

MEADOWLARK: What you scattin at me?

GERRY: He means unless you are a personal friend of the Home Secretary you're on your way out this afternoon. Going back sonny what it mean.

RAYMOND: Mr Warner, have you got the sum of £102·68?

MEADOWLARK: I never would be here jawing with yeh two white asses eff a had, why?

RAYMOND: I am obliged to ask you to pay for your own fare.

MEADOWLARK: Where dis fare going tekk me, Siberian Moscow?

RAYMOND: You are being taken aboard Caribbean Airways 14·50 hours flight to Jamaica.

MEADOWLARK: Yeh figures been wrong yeh know. Cost at least too huner'n ninety-five – return fly by International Airport, Montego Bay.

GERRY: It's a one-way ticket.

MEADOWLARK: Am I tinkin of takin a first-class up front, me hans runnin up an down de bottle of free Cap'n Davy brown rum and lemonade.

RAYMOND: I don't think so.

MEADOWLARK: Is a cryin shame – eff yeh offered every black Jamaican a free weekend an all in de Jamaican Hilton Hotel, an a bottle of rum for the flight, yeh'd solve the British racial problem in no time at all.

RAYMOND: I'm to understand you have not got £102·68 on you, Mr Warner?

MEADOWLARK: Yeh catchin up wit I fast.

RAYMOND: I am further obliged to tell you then that the Home Secretary will treat this fare paid in advance as a loan, which you will be required to repay in the eventuality of your returning here. This money comes from a sum set aside for such eventualities and is supplied at the discretion of the Treasury.

MEADOWLARK: Yeh can tell his Home Secretary I is obliged den for his generous ways of tinkin of helpin poor old Meadowlark his ole black-eye chum you know. But a don't see at all how it is a can go.

GERRY: You must be joking. You can't draw breath and take it with you without our permission, boy.

MEADOWLARK: Ent nuffin say a can't stay if yeh tekk a sudden liken an all an had me adopted is dere?

GERRY: I have absolutely no intention of adopting you, son.

MEADOWLARK: Ent nuffin say a can't stay here eff a just about on the day of my wedding day, mon?

GERRY: Wedding day. You're full of shit.

MEADOWLARK: Am tinking arl mekk yeh eat I shit.

GERRY: Want me to have you for resisting order of deportation an threatening behaviour boy!

MEADOWLARK: Nuffin yeh cen do me. En nuffin say I can't stay a wed a girl from dis country you know!

RAYMOND: That lady you were with this morning –

MEADOWLARK: Year mon ent no lady mon es my girl an a want teh marry her legal an all now.

RAYMOND: When were these banns put up?

MEADOWLARK: Three weeks ago word a goh en de lordie praise I fer heffin de wit!

GERRY: Old-fashioned natural godgiven bullshitter Ray. Come on – let's finish it – I've got a match this afternoon.

RAYMOND [to MEADOWLARK]: What evidence have you? You intend going through with this ceremony?

[IRENE *knocks loudly on the door. She pushes her way past* GERRY *into the office. She carries a suitcase and a huge transparent polythene bag filled with multi-coloured woolly tops. She is wearing something white in the way of a wedding look and being nice and refreshing to look at with the ring on her finger.*]

IRENE: Here I am . . . Where is he? What you doing with my Meadowlark?

GERRY: Out you! This is the interview room. No unauthorized personnel –

IRENE: Hallo Meadowlark! . . . Lovey!

GERRY: I'm telling you! This place ain't for appy families, girl. Am I going to toss you out?

IRENE: Shove off, greasey!

GERRY [*pulling* IRENE]: Right! Out! Into my office! You want to see *that* – ave to ask me first! And I've got a few questions too! Off!

[IRENE *has time to push the bag of woolly tops towards* MEADOWLARK.]

IRENE: Leave this then! It's all his! Grease off smarmbag!

[GERRY *bundles her out of the door and slams the door.*]

Meadowlark!

[*He turns back.*]

RAYMOND: If you want me to understand your position at this eleventh hour I want certain facts from you. Are you going to cooperate? I don't think, in any way, it has entered your head just how serious a matter deportation is. At this juncture I am your last resort. And I have an inch space left to me in which I can arbitrate if I see your particular case has not had proper hearing. Nevertheless, what you are suggesting to me – the idea of a valid marriage at the last minute – is, courtesy of Immigration rules HC 80 paras 26 and 26a, not insufficient to mount appeal by virtue of becoming a British subject.

MEADOWLARK: Am losin almost every word yeh comin on me with, don't want all dis goat-beard gumble mouthin tell I de truth you know . . .

RAYMOND: Mr Warner. If you can prove to me you had intent to marry before today, then there is a tiny possibility courtesy of an amended subsection which can, at least, delay the deportation procedure.

MEADOWLARK: Am saying to meself dis is de great day of me life whent a waked an a looked out my window in mornin I'm goah beat up Babylon an heff me honeymoon tonight an yeh comin round meh ways of tinkin a appreciate.

RAYMOND: I beg your pardon?

MEADOWLARK: A lekk yeh shit, a say.

RAYMOND: I consider it my duty to stick to the rule of the law, but with consideration for those who appear to be victims of this law, Mr Warner.

MEADOWLARK: Am sharin yeh bus ticket en that one.

RAYMOND: But I want the truth.

MEADOWLARK: A swear en book yeh please, a got de banns, a done all deh arrangementize, it was mean teh be a big secret, an when ma girl arrive, a tekk her straight off to the ceremony at 2·30 dis afternoon. Am truth shitmon.

RAYMOND: How long have these banns been up?

MEADOWLARK: Dis is three weeks teh the day.

RAYMOND: And where was the ceremony to be?

MEADOWLARK: Churchplace mon en Arkwright Road, Brixton. Just as yeh comin round de corner from me.

RAYMOND: What is the name of the vicar?

MEADOWLARK: He's am priestman. Very liberal en he's torts.

RAYMOND: But the day and time was fixed?

MEADOWLARK: Fixed for today, mon, an at the hour a tell an the churchplace down at 15 Arkwright Road, teh SW2. Telephone Mistah Brucknell, 732–5081. Teh Missers Brucknell en dere too. Me word on it, now, never dare tell a lie against the churchman, mon. So why don yeh phone him now.

RAYMOND: All right Mr Warner. We'll telephone him together if you'll just follow me.

[*They exit to stage right office. Behind glass panels stage left.*]

IRENE: It's here. It's here. I know it's here.

GERRY: Have you got a passport or haven't you?

IRENE: Of course I have. Here it is. OK!

GERRY [*he laughs*]: Yeh, that's OK.

[*Lights up in stage right office.*]

MEADOWLARK: Mr Brucknell forgive me for calling you so early. This is Mr Warner here. Mr M. R. Warner. Apropos the wedding this afternoon. Everything's fine sir. But I'm having a little problem with my business arrangements. My fiancée and I are here but we're in such a hurry. You see I hafta take a plane from Gatwick Airport almost the moment we're married. I wonder Mr Brucknell would you be kind enough to do the ceremony here.

[*to* RAYMOND] Yeh have to make as if yer talkin the Queen's language with she priestman . . . I'm in the offices at Gatwick Airport, Mr Brucknell. I'm in a desperate hurry for this, see. Something come up, and I just can't leave the airport all day. And my business become an urgent matter, so urgent, fact is my life depend on it.

. . . You don't have any other weddings? Will I pay your bus fare out here? Course, Mr Brucknell. You'll come out for half-past two sharp? I'm extremely grateful, sir. Super.

[RAYMOND *gesticulates he'd like to speak on the phone.*]

. . . Hold on Mr Brucknell. My friend the gentleman other side of the desk here wants a word with you, hold on. I'll see you at 2·30 prompt, sir – I don't want him ter tink arm some half-bred badass Nigerian nigger juicin de palm wine craze an talkin red lobster seafood rubbish back teh Africa roots, mon. Eff yeh see . . .

RAYMOND. Quite.

[MEADOWLARK *hands the phone back to* RAYMOND.]

RAYMOND [*in phone*]: . . . Good morning Mr Brucknell. My name is Borrall. I am an officer in the Appeals Office, Immigration, at Gatwick. Mr Warner, although it is not for me to divulge details of his legal standing, has a small problem with his passport here at Gatwick, and we cannot say when we'll be through with the documents. Meanwhile, I understand you have already notified your congregation of his banns for a wedding ceremony today, and it is not my intention to stand in the way of this happy occasion. You are prepared to come out here for the Service? Yes, sir, you ask for the Office of Appeals, Immigration Centre, in the East Block. Thank you.

[*Puts phone down.*

RAYMOND *stares thoughtfully at* MEADOWLARK. MEADOWLARK *wriggles a little.*

GERRY *breezes back in all smiles. He slaps* MEADOWLARK *on the shoulder. Shakes his hand.*]

GERRY: All ready then? See your fiancée? Sort out the endbits? I haven't asked my colleague Raymond here, but if you want any extra little help with this wedding then, like a couple of humble witnesses well – you can count on Raymond and me.

RAYMOND: Eh . . . let's not rush into irregular grey areas.

GERRY [*to* RAYMOND]: I'll tell you later, mate. [*To* MEADOWLARK]: You come with me chum, and your Irene is waiting down the corridor for you.

MEADOWLARK [*amazed at* GERRY's *friendliness*]: Yeh bin hidin in the Gatwick VIP lounge bottlefeedin export whisky, mon? You en sound like teh fellah walked out dis door moment ago.

GERRY [*breezily*]: This way, Meadowlark!

[MEADOWLARK *grabs his big bag of coloured woolly tops.* IRENE *is sitting in the large office centre.* GERRY *fetches* MEADOWLARK *forward.* GERRY *is beaming.*]

IRENE: Meadowlark.

MEADOWLARK [*to* GERRY]: And why are yeh grinnin lekk Philharmonic grand pianoforte keyboard . . . ?

GERRY [*leaving*]: You're got boy. By your short and teaming ugly curlies, you are.

MEADOWLARK [*after* GERRY *leaves*]: What he done darlin bin rapin yeh when meh back is turn?

GERRY: I want the door left ajar.

IRENE: My darling husband!

MEADOWLARK: We not quite dere yet, yeh know. I catch a glimpse in that mother's eye just minute ago – something schemin in dere.

IRENE: You swear you meant it? That this is the day?

MEADOWLARK: Am putting meh hand on I heart.

IRENE: Yeh ain't backin down?

MEADOWLARK: Yeh got teh ring ent yeh?

IRENE: I want to hear you say it.

MEADOWLARK: Now darlin, a tink arv already asked yeh.

IRENE: No, it was me who asked you. Remember? We got caught up top of that fairground sky-wheel on Clapham Common, and there was an electric cable fault, and I didn't want to die.

MEADOWLARK: Well anyways one ob we did it!

IRENE: I want to hear it now?

MEADOWLARK: Irene! . . . Fock it . . . Will yeh tekk yourself teh be ma wife you know – ? An all dat crap, mon.

IRENE: I do. So help me.

MEADOWLARK: No Irene darlin yeh save tat for de service in teh afternoon an –

[*She hugs and kisses him. He is propelled back.*]

IRENE: . . . Ain't it great? Aren't you happy! I'm over the moon. Wait till mum finds out! Give us a smile Meadowlark please!

MEADOWLARK: I catch a glimpse in dat mother's eye. Am thinkin I got dem suspicions . . . someting not quite in place, you know.

IRENE: Everything is ready. I've got my suitcase packed.

You've got your bag of woolly tops. And all I've got to do is pay my bit of the fare. And that's no problem.

MEADOWLARK: Am not tinking bout no fockin honeymoon. Costs are mountin in the hotel and catering trade.

IRENE: We can have just a little honeymoon. I don't care if it's a park bench.

MEADOWLARK: We can heff a six-pack of Red Stripe if yeh like, en coupla extra Jamaican pattis after teh Catford races, and at all!

IRENE: We're not going to Catford dog-track you idiot. We're taking a plane straight after the service.

MEADOWLARK: A ent got money take no plane nowhere for a honeymoon, Irene.

IRENE: Meadowlark it only costs £23 single for me, and it's free for you, so what are you complaining about?

MEADOWLARK: En who's payin for me en some plane, de British Government, mon? You crazy like.

IRENE: Course they pay! I've just talked to that bloke Gerry. He says he arranges the cost immediately. Ain't no skin off of his, is it!

MEADOWLARK: Dat man Gerry blue nose meany? What are yeh sayin teh me!

IRENE: Gerry says he is delighted to arrange it for this afternoon. As soon as we are married.

MEADOWLARK: Am smellin a rat.

IRENE: A what?

MEADOWLARK: Dat Gerry who was grinnin lekk pianoforte?

IRENE: Yes.

MEADOWLARK: En says he's puttin me on a plane going where?

IRENE: Dublin you fool!

MEADOWLARK: Doblin! Where de focks dat!

IRENE: In Ireland you cloth-eared Cocoa!

MEADOWLARK: Am never heard of no Doblin. Am in what Ireland you tokkin about!

IRENE: Dublin you black moron is the capital of the Republic of Ireland. You know next door in the sea like, bit further past Pontin's Holiday Camp at Aberdovey!

MEADOWLARK: Am not goin to no honeymoon in Doblin, heff yeh idea how much the bed and breakfast is cost dere! Mon, it's heavy. En how'm a fetchin yer back? Ay?

IRENE: Meadowlark it isn't exactly going there for our honeymoon just the honeymoon alone like.

MEADOWLARK: It en?

IRENE: No, I'm talking about something very serious, now.

MEADOWLARK: Well what the ras yeh scattin on?

IRENE: I had a very nice conversation with that fellah –

MEADOWLARK: Dat blue nark Gerry?

IRENE: An this is what he advises. Because there ain't no other way doing it.

MEADOWLARK: Slow down now . . . dat fellah say what?

IRENE: He said there was no need for Her Majesty's Treasurer to send you all the way to Jamaica, when it would be cheaper to send you to Dublin.

MEADOWLARK: Who de fokk he tink he am! No one ask me about Doblin. Dis Doblin en Ireland?

IRENE: Yes.

MEADOWLARK: Ireland den where dos Irish people folks commin frem?

IRENE: Yes.

MEADOWLARK: Mon, heff yeh ev bin to dis Ireland? Em noffin but streets full of potato-eatin people wid big ears and green eyes mon, walkin along de pavemen talking dere tongues off drinkin dat warm black goat sweat beer wid de white froth'n, mon! Dat sufferin Ireland for yeh.

IRENE: I know. I was born in Dublin. I lived in Belfast.

MEADOWLARK: De ras!

IRENE: So that's why – after we're married – we've got to go to Dublin.

MEADOWLARK: Yeh not gettin thru to de brain matter, honey.

IRENE: Meadowlark you've got nowhere else to go! For God's sake – they throwing you out the country!

MEADOWLARK: Calm down dere . . . cool it down . . . now . . . what am Doblin an going to rassin Doblin ter do with I an yer?

IRENE [*softly*]: We are about to be married. The vicar's coming here ain't he?

MEADOWLARK: Is comin.

IRENE: Well then. As soon as the marriage is over, that bloke Gerry and the other bloke, will put you on a plane for free for nothin you git this afternoon for Dublin with me your wife.

MEADOWLARK: Am not followin de thread.

IRENE: Because I am Irish. I have a valid Irish passport, and you'll be able to take out Republic of Ireland nationality because you are Mister Me. And I'm Missus You! See?

[MEADOWLARK *quietens. He has to lead her up the path. Has to finish it his way*.]

MEADOWLARK: Yeh mean yer tryin tell I you en no English girl at all?

IRENE: I'm an Irish colleen.

MEADOWLARK: Yeh mean yer marrying me under false pretences?

IRENE: I haven't married you yet!

MEADOWLARK: Irene listen teh me – what colour is your passport?

IRENE [*produces it*]: Green . . . look.

MEADOWLARK: It en blue?

IRENE [*under his nose*]: Bloody green, are you colour-blind?

MEADOWLARK: En blue all right . . . aawww burn de skies en goh beat up Babylon, mon, is big trouble comin up quick, an beat all a we!

IRENE: I don't understand.

MEADOWLARK: De weddin's off!

IRENE: Shit on you!

MEADOWLARK: Am off, darlin. A loves yeh. But am off. Ats de flat end of de tin edge.

IRENE: I'm going to tear your eyes out!

MEADOWLARK: Shudup. Am tinkin.

IRENE: You changed your mind! You bloody can't! You did it in front of witnesses! Down Coldharbour you black shit! We're getting wed!

MEADOWLARK: Am workin on it.

IRENE: I've bleedin scraped, Meadowlark, keeping you, Meadowlark, month in month out, you git, fucking don't turn round on me and change your bitching black head first one way 'Yes we will' then other 'No we won't'. I come to the end.

MEADOWLARK: Shudup. Meh mind is concentratin.

IRENE: If you back down on me now I'll sue you! For false whatever! I was promised, man, and you stick to it so help me I'll hand you a cut-glass jam patti in the teeth!

MEADOWLARK: I got big problem.

IRENE: What do you think my mother's been thinking all these months – when I write her and tell her what you are – at least now you've got a chance to prove my mother wrong.

MEADOWLARK: En met your rarssin mudder.

IRENE: She died the death when she heard what colour your nose is!

MEADOWLARK: I unable to convince yeh a don't give a fart in a bugle factory bout your famous mother.

IRENE [*quieter*]: I was a Catholic virgin when I first met you.

MEADOWLARK: En tru.

IRENE: I saved all my money and cooked your meals and bought them and paid the gas meter and did the electricity bills, and bloody choked to death on green bananas and yam pickle. I've sacrificed my life to you. Now I'm all ready and prepared, take you home, give up everything here, no work for me in Dublin, tell you that, and all for what? To keep you in the dingy style what you thieving accustomed to!

MEADOWLARK: Yeh was sleepin wid two Pakistani brothers, when a picked yeh up an rescued yer from an overdose of curried cat food in the Locarno, Streatham, on a Saturday night. En no virgin.

IRENE: Pakistanis are gentlemen, that's more'n –

MEADOWLARK: Pakis just dogs an cats Indians heff yeh ever see a Paki tekk a bath?

IRENE: I want to know exactly where I stand?

MEADOWLARK: Darlin, a en goin to fockin Doblin, an ats flat. Is freezin the ass off me cold in Doblin. En no Irish black boys a can sell woolly tops to en Doblin. Am trying to mekk an honest living you know. A can't understand word those Irish freaks sayin gibberygoosh mon. Am British thru an thru.

IRENE: Are we goin to wed like you said in front of those men like?

MEADOWLARK: Darlin yeh know what I'm lekk. I tell you one ting den I turn around am de other ting up front with the lights winkin. Yeh know my philosophy – two fish in de sky better'n one bird in der sea. Kindating. Yeh don truly love I.

IRENE: That's the trouble . . .!

MEADOWLARK: Because a rescued yeh from couple Pakis poisoning yeh with hot cat food – yeh don't truly love I.

IRENE: Yes . . .

MEADOWLARK: Yeh hate me am yeh stinking thieving lying Meadowlark who been livin off yeh.

IRENE: That's right . . .

MEADOWLARK: Cheatin an whoring and sleeping with black girls behind yeh back . . .

IRENE [*sharpish*]: When was that?

MEADOWLARK: An tekkin money from yeh purse every opportunity an stealin yeh wages an none of yeh white friends'll tekk to me. Yeh hate me, Irene.

IRENE: No . . .

MEADOWLARK: I en no good for nuffin. Yeh despise I for what am teh real let go I.

IRENE: I . . . want to know if we're going to Catford tonight, that's all, for the dog-track?

MEADOWLARK: Yeh know a can't do that. Am on meh way out, girl. I had it, mon.
[*She holds back a moment. She reaches for her suitcase, picks it up and then slams it on to the floor, she jumps on it then pummels it. She rolls on to the floor beside it in tears.*]
. . . Yeh feelin better?
[*She shakes her head negatively.*]
. . . It's all done now then, Irene.
[*She nods her head in assent.*]

... Never did love yeh much anyway. You know?
[*She nods.*]
... Yeh hatin meh now, darlin.
[*She nods. Yes, she is. Lots of tears and shaking.
She stands up and goes to the door.*]

IRENE: ... What's goin to happen to you then?

MEADOWLARK: Oh a got a little fish in de sky somewhere fetch me the luck an all.

IRENE: ... Trra.

MEADOWLARK: Ooh! ... A forget yeh still holdin on teh me wedding ring, Irene. Yeh don't want keep that, then.

IRENE: ... Course not.
[*She pulls it off her finger and hands it back to him.*]

MEADOWLARK [*backing away*]: ... Cheerybyes den, Irene. An ... it's been great times an all ...
[*She exits.*]

GERRY: ... Hallo where's your future bride then?

MEADOWLARK: Don spit on me, whitey!

GERRY: Me? Me what doing you the favours? Me? The witness and all like?

MEADOWLARK: Bleddy knew yeh did en no time at all dat girl en no use to meh!

GERRY: Has she changed her mind then?

MEADOWLARK: Yeh bleddy knew a weren't goin to Doblin, Ireland. That was why you is smilin like shit. A see de light on that one.

GERRY: What was it – b.o. – you smell a bit like the old goat cheese you do. Sniff, sniff!

MEADOWLARK: Are yeh makin racist remarks?

GERRY: No.

MEADOWLARK: Am tinkin yeh a raving white bigot now.

GERRY: We gotta have a yoke somehow ein yoke ay? Now – you tell me what's your problem?

MEADOWLARK: Am no bleddy going to Doblin.

GERRY: Fair enough. Where would you like to go to?

MEADOWLARK: Am bleddy goin back home.

GERRY: To sunny Jamaica?

MEADOWLARK: To bleddy sunny Coldharbour Lane, Brixton, yeh whitey rars.

GERRY: Take a bet on that?

MEADOWLARK: Yeh is offerin odds?

GERRY: Yeh, if you like.

RAYMOND: Mr Warner we've come to the end of the road. I don't know what you intended to do after this marriage ceremony which was to be, but I am left with no alternative but to proceed according to my instructions.

MEADOWLARK [to GERRY]: Yeh lovin it!

GERRY: Fellah – I'm on your side, matey.

MEADOWLARK: Eff yeh on my side who me enemies den?!

RAYMOND: It is clear to me, although you intended to marry this Miss –?

GERRY: Connor. Irene Connor.

RAYMOND: As soon as you were appraised of the fact that she only possesses an Irish passport, you changed your wedding plans.

MEADOWLARK: En weddin some family of Irish potato pickers. Dey sleepin in wet beds wid black bog bricks in der firegrate an all the soot climbin up yeh nose cetch yeh death of tuberculosis.

RAYMOND: Whatever your personal motives, I have to make a record of these details.

MEADOWLARK: Goah write it all down, en weddin no Irish virgin, en so much of a virgin come to tink. When a got dere a find two Pakistanis bin dere en front of me soilin up de pitch, already.

RAYMOND [writing]: You are not marrying this Miss Connor?

MEADOWLARK: No, sir, ain't.

RAYMOND: And you object to being sent to Ireland.

MEADOWLARK: Put yeh socks and y-front nickers on dat.

RAYMOND: And this wedding you planned is now cancelled?

MEADOWLARK: No, a never said that.

RAYMOND [writing]: And you can offer no further objection to this proposed flight to Jamaica which the Home Secretary is empowered to put in motion.

MEADOWLARK: A never said dat, neither.

GERRY [*watching* RAYMOND *write*]: Ray . . .

RAYMOND: What?

GERRY [*tapping his nose*]: Big smelly evil rat coming up.

MEADOWLARK: A never said no weddin off, man.

GERRY: Look Cocoa –

MEADOWLARK: Meadowlark I right name –

GERRY: Without this girl, there is no wedding. Without wedding you got your marching orders. Given your marching orders there ain't not a blue thing you can do in the yonder cloudless!

RAYMOND: Am I to understand you have another proposal by way of appeal against this warrant for deportation?

MEADOWLARK: No man, am stickin with the *gloo* of de first.

RAYMOND: *Gloo?*

MEADOWLARK: Stickin to the spirit of de first ting yeh see. *Gloo* is de spirit yer know. The spirit of de appeal.

GERRY [*to* MEADOWLARK]: Spit it out then, son.

MEADOWLARK: Yeh see . . . a don't think yeh ever asked I what a was doin in my room dis mornin.

GERRY: What were you doing in your room this morning?

MEADOWLARK: A was on de point of sayin to Irene, dis is de greatest day of meh life. An, eff yeh hadn't turned up like that, shoutin bout arrests and warrants an ting, Irene an me was finished. That was the end of our thing, yeh know. A don't love Irene, Irene all in de past. It was a sorta cheerybye Irene, an tat was dat. Irene an me used to live together. Then we split up an in no time at all a was meetin her by chance, usually on Fridays when she had a little money in she purse after the pay day, an a took her out den – or she took me out den – depending on whether she tooks her purse with her when we . . . all de time a knew et was over and done wit. So's by the off-chance I lyin in bed wid Irene en yeh come crashin in like dis, en scaring me to death with all this official paper shit, mon am terrified like, an running all over me mout not knowin what I'm sayin from minute to minute. I'm caught the shit scared in me an ma eyeballs goin from side to side, an meh armpits sweating up. Yeh got to understand meh way of tinkin. So a said in de heat of the moment 'Marry me Irene!' Meanin, 'Please for Christ's sake stick with me, kid, tese horseflies bitin I to the he bone marrer.'

RAYMOND [*to* GERRY]: What is he saying?

MEADOWLARK: Am sayin, look, lekk here, yeh see this bag with the woolly tops. A got woolly top for Charlton colours when dey at home. An a got woolly top for Arsenal, see, an for Chelsea, and for Tottenham den en case a don't find nuff niggers down the north bank, a go up the far pitch, and eff day all come down frem Liverpool – a get out the Liverpool woollies . . .

GERRY [*to* RAYMOND]: He's saying he sells these things to either group of supporters either end of the pitch. In other words he's –

MEADOWLARK: Doin two fish in de sky better'n one bird in the sea.

RAYMOND: I see. You earn your living by selling these ear-mittens at football matches –

MEADOWLARK: An don't forget de cricket too. Anywhere's black kids want one dey see me. Bin a jolly good trade been so far. So dats what am sayin bout two fish in the sky stead of de one bird.

RAYMOND: These ear-mittens –

MEADOWLARK: En no ear-mittens, they is woolly tams. The white kids is always runnin down the streets stealin woolly tops off of nigger heads, an am always comin up behind with new ones ter kepp level with de rising demand en an insatiable market.

[*Holds one up* –]

Irene ent the girl a intended to wed.

GERRY: Yes she is, I heard you propose to her. This morning.

MEADOWLARK: Just cos a was runnin scared.

GERRY: Am I allowed to inquire who the lucky girl is then?

RAYMOND: I think I'm entering into a grey area here.

MEADOWLARK: She's called Edna. She's called Edna Walter, an she is de one.

GERRY: You're full of crap, Cocoa.

RAYMOND: Where is this Edna Walter?

MEADOWLARK: She comin.

RAYMOND: I asked you, Mr Warner, where is she?

MEADOWLARK: She comin here today.

GERRY: How can she possibly be coming to Gatwick Airport you nana, when nobody knows you're here but that – that Irene! You lying black knot.

MEADOWLARK: She comin.

RAYMOND: How? Mr Warner?

MEADOWLARK: She arrivin on the twelve-thirty flight, Caribbean Airways.

RAYMOND: At Gatwick!

MEADOWLARK: Sure enough.

RAYMOND: With what purpose in mind?

MEADOWLARK: She goin wed me yeh white stiff! She en comin here to shake yeh hand a never heard her tell me.

GERRY [to RAYMOND]: Lying through his teeth.

RAYMOND [to MEADOWLARK]: She's comin here today in order to proceed with this ceremony you have put out the banns for?

MEADOWLARK: Yes am tellin yeh now!

RAYMOND: In what way does this marriage to Miss Walter in any way alter the grounds of this deportation order?

MEADOWLARK: Edna Briddish tru an tru.

RAYMOND: . . . How British?

MEADOWLARK: Very Briddish. She was here for ten days yer kno durin the Jubilee celebrations. Am very keen on de royal Queen Betty you know. A used to sell flags all along de Mall kindating. Anyway, dats de truth am tellin.

RAYMOND: Your *British* fiancée has only lived in this country ten days?

MEADOWLARK: First time she ever saw merry old England, yearh.

RAYMOND: Where for the rest of her *British* life has she lived?

MEADOWLARK: Guyana. She been born in Georgetown, an she comin here to wed me now, an all.

GERRY: What colour skin is she?

MEADOWLARK: Black, see, just black lekk me.

RAYMOND: And she is going to marry you here. And you are prepared to fly back to Guyana with her? I see.

MEADOWLARK: Oh no, see. Am stayin here den. So's she.

RAYMOND: On what grounds?

MEADOWLARK: You awful thick yeh know. Edna more British than you man. She's got a British passport! Like you man! A big blue one!

GERRY [*breathing deeply*]: Fuck me . . .

MEADOWLARK: Be a big pleasure mon any time yeh wan.
   [GERRY *and* RAYMOND *exchange glances. A pause.*]
So den who got who by de short an curlies, now am tinkin ay?

GERRY: Mind your nose, son, I can put it out of joint.

MEADOWLARK: Threatening to beat me up and insult me on account racial hatred am hearin?

RAYMOND [*tersely to* GERRY]: Mr Warner almost has a point there, Mr Radinski.

MEADOWLARK: An what kind of name is dat? Radinski? Is Polish or am a Chinaman. Is bleddy not true blue British stake a woolly top on at.

GERRY: Don't pass your old rope on me. I know what you are!

MEADOWLARK: I a hypocrite, I a lying cheat, I a sponger, I a dirty bastard what livin off of women, an floggin two woolly tops either end of the stadium, an keepin two fish in de sky stead of one bird in the sea, always broke, man, always runnin, tryin to cheat de honest public, tekkin de easy way out, snitchin a quid here, an hustlin one dere, never stop watchin where de main chance! Right?

GERRY: You said it.

MEADOWLARK: An how do ye tink a come by dat way? En who did the learning?

GERRY: Bottom of the barrel, mate.

MEADOWLARK: Bottom bottom badass naked bottom of de barrel, man. Right?

GERRY: Fucking on!

MEADOWLARK: But in meh case deres a difference. En Meadowlark it seem worse, cos old Meadowlark bad bottom of the shit heap so he am, he am black into de bargain a never heard you mention dat! Eff a was rassclatt badass barrel bottom whitey shit hoo ha an hell suck eggs shit a wouldn't be in dis disutation! Boy when yer see a bad black'un it stick in yeh gut don't it till yer forget yer ev heard of a bad white'un. Yes, sir. Eff a wasn't funny yer know ... eff a hadn't dis langidge come out a bit twisted in me talkin ... eff shit an shit an shit kindating be a different song yerd be singin, yer may mekk up yer sufferin mind on dat!

RAYMOND: Are you asking us to grant you the same facilities in terms of time and extension of privileges, as we did over the eh first young woman? Mr Warner?

MEADOWLARK: Aw ... am stuffed up to the throat wid yer. Don't want no privilege. Just give me Edna. En noffin else.

RAYMOND: I have to observe the letter of the law. According to subsection –

MEADOWLARK: Am bad. Real bad ole Meadowlark. Right?

RAYMOND: I will grant you the necessary facilities if you ask for them, properly.

MEADOWLARK: Am asking den aren I?

GERRY: This Edna don't exist. It's a waste of time.

MEADOWLARK: Am de worst old rope 'nigger' yer ev met? Right?

GERRY: Lock him up in the large room until his Jamaica flight is called.

MEADOWLARK: Am cheatin an lyin dere is no Edna dere is no priestman dere is nuffin but the white paper forms front of your nose, true word baby?!

GERRY [to RAYMOND]: Come on Ray, call it a day.

MEADOWLARK: At right. Wipe yeh hands of me.

RAYMOND [to MEADOWLARK]: Nothing you have said or done invalidates your right to appeal against this order under subsection 15, Immigration Appeal Act (69), on the grounds of extenuating claims for a certificate of status. I will stand by that.

MEADOWLARK [*looking confused*]: An I too, sir, man.

GERRY: Meaning I'm not getting to my football match this afternoon.

MEADOWLARK: An I too, you know.

GERRY: It's going to be an all afternoon job then?

RAYMOND [*looking at his watch*]: I'm at eh . . . five past twelve.

GERRY [*looking at his*]: Funny . . . one minute to. Must be losing.

RAYMOND [*to* MEADOWLARK]: It was Caribbean Airways, Mr Warner?

MEADOWLARK: Man yer sound as if yeh don't believe a word a say!

[LIGHTS.

From another direction a busy tannoy system puts out a message.]

TANNOY [*V.O.*]: Miss Edna Walter please. Miss Edna Walter. Disembarking Flight 06974. Will Miss Walter please report to the Caribbean Airways desk where there is an urgent message. Miss Edna Walter . . .

[*Later.* RAYMOND *and* GERRY *sit in the main office centre.* GERRY *pulls out a couple of beers from a zip-side of his bag.* RAYMOND *looks disapproving.*

In the centre of the stage right office sits MEADOWLARK. *Very much alone.*]

GERRY [*offering the beer*]: Go on man, live a little, stretch the rules a little.

RAYMOND [*shaking his head*]: Thank you.

GERRY: Ray don't worry, I'm telling you she won't be on that plane. I had a pal working on the dockside immigration with me. C. and E., Dover. Some time back. He'd caught this Mauritian lad just after he'd got wed to a British girl. They cosied up in the Wee Willie Winkie motel, on the Maidstone Road. They were straight into it an all. Passion honeymoon chitchat. And my pal just handed the deskbloke a big tip to give him the room number. He's creeping up to their door.

With his warrant in his hand for the lad. Suddenly, there's this ridiculous pidgin English lovebit goin on inside. He hasn't the heart, my pal. He's frozen to the carpet. Inside – 'Me darlin ting I cenn ardly avin beliv it yor lovely face is all *mine*.' And – 'darlin tweet, I cenn ardly beliv your lovely white neck all *mine*.' And – 'Tweet tweet, I cenn hardly beliv tose roun pink perfect titties with the red splots all *mine* now.' And so on, you know. My pal, not having the heart to be rough on them, yelled through the keyhole – 'Oi! Begging yours, mate, but when you get down to the deportation warrant I've slid under the door; that one's bloody *mine*!'

RAYMOND: I think, after all, I will have that beer. After that appalling story, Mr Radinski.

GERRY: Frankly, if I inquired too far back into where my old lot comes from, believe you me I'd get a few warrants unearthed I would. Awful lot of Poles, Polski yids and Polski commies, crept ashore turn of the century like. Where you born Ray?

RAYMOND: I beg your pardon!

GERRY: Datchett? Wapping? Herne Bay on Sea?

RAYMOND: Isle of Dogs if you must know.

GERRY: Oh yes. In the Pacific is that?

RAYMOND: On the north bank of the Thames. It's an island peninsula as a matter of fact. Right opposite Greenwich.

GERRY: You're a bloody foreigner you are. You got a passport for coming off there!

RAYMOND: My father worked the whole of the First World War on Nightwatch in the old Rotherhithe Maritime Company. Those boats were kept loaded with the Spar Torpedoes for Class B subs. Every night he had to sign in and sign out a Webley-Fosberry automatic revolver.

GERRY: Tell you what Ray? I'll give you ten to one this Edna Walter from Guyana don't exist?

RAYMOND: No.

GERRY: I give you a hundred to one.

RAYMOND: I'm afraid I never bet. It's a family rule. Sorry. I'm glad you mentioned Mauritians just now. I have nothing against them. Rather charming lot. It's their passport drives me in a twist. It's identical to true brit blue. Did you notice ever? We've twice stamped Mauritians out of the British gate with no visa whatsoever in the past month. In the dark you're in a hurry. Late at night. There must be a fair number of Mauritians walking around the place with open-ended entry stamps on non-patrial passports.

GERRY: You got a funny mind you have, Ray, it's all filled with twisted up bits of old paper. You need a hobby, mate, keep you cheerful. Cheers!

[*Just as* RAYMOND *lifts his glass of beer, we hear sharp heels along a corridor.* RAYMOND *and* GERRY *look up. The heels approach. A rap on the door. And* EDNA WALTER *enters. She carries a shoulder bag. She has that sudden fazed air of a girl who has just got off the plane.*]

EDNA: I'm Miss Walter. What is it you want with me? Is something wrong?

[*They stare at her.*
Blackout for five seconds.
Later.]

RAYMOND: . . . Now, Miss Walter.

EDNA: I want to see Meadowlark! Where is he?

GERRY: No problem at all, love, just let's get all the answers written down –

EDNA: I'll give you the answers when I've heard the questions.

RAYMOND: Place of birth, Miss Walter?

EDNA: Mackenzie British Military Hospital, Mackenzie, Guyana. Why?

RAYMOND: Date?

EDNA: 4 May 1956.

RAYMOND: Parents' nationality?

EDNA: British passport holders. Resident in Guyana. My father was a civil servant for many years in Government House.

RAYMOND: What language do you speak?

EDNA: English, of course. And fluent Dutch. I was educated on the Corentyne River at a Methodist school. The first language on the Surinam side of the river is Dutch. And I have good command of Talkie Talkie.

RAYMOND: I beg your pardon?

EDNA: The native dialect is a mixture of early English and Afro pidgin, based on the old imperialist colonial plantation rule.

RAYMOND: You possess a UK passport? Of course.

[*She fetches it out.*]

EDNA: Of course.

GERRY: Of course.

[*As* RAYMOND *quickly leafs through the passport.*]

RAYMOND: How long have you known Mr Warner?

EDNA: None of your damned business.

GERRY: The man's only trying to be helpful, ducks.

EDNA: I'll be the judge of that.

RAYMOND: What is the purpose of your trip here?

EDNA: My father received a letter from Mr Warner three months back, asking for permission to marry me. I hope to marry Mr Warner as soon as I can.

GERRY: Have you had any financial dealings with Mr Warner?

EDNA: Are you serious?

RAYMOND: You intend to stay here how long?

EDNA: I have a business efficiency pass from the University of Paramaribe, Surinam. I am also a qualified shorthand typist. I intend to find work here.

RAYMOND [*smiling steel*]: Nevertheless – all this serves no purpose at all, if by marrying Mr Warner you think you can supply him with an umbrella for patrial status. Under the amended Commonwealth Immigrants Act (1971) you must show parents born in this country, Miss Walter.

EDNA [*very cool*]: My grandmother and my grandfather were born and raised in Liverpool before they returned home to Georgetown, in 1938. I think you'll find this allows me free status in Britain under terms governed by the NCCI.

RAYMOND [*slightly rattled*]: The what?

EDNA: National Council for Commonwealth Immigrants.

GERRY: Been reading all your books haven't you, ducks?

EDNA: I want to see Mr Warner now.

RAYMOND: You'll be taken to see Mr Warner when I am finished with these inquiries. And not till then.

EDNA: And I want to know why I have been brought here. And I want to know why you are holding Mr Warner in this building?

RAYMOND: I am empowered by the Immigration Act '71, under the schedule dealing with deportation administration.

EDNA: And who is being deported?

RAYMOND: I have in front of me an order of deportation for Mr Meadowlark Rachel Warner.

EDNA: On what grounds?

RAYMOND: That information is classified confidential.

EDNA: Oh come on, who are you kidding? I'm his fiancée.

RAYMOND: Have you more than £150 in your possession?

EDNA: Mind your own damned business.

RAYMOND: Have you a return flight ticket to Georgetown in your possession?

EDNA: I won't answer.

RAYMOND: Have you the name and address of an acquaintance in Britain who can vouch for your good character?

GERRY: Excluding Meadowlark you see.

EDNA: I'm not speaking.

RAYMOND: Miss Walter, I don't think you understand how thoroughly the Immigration Office here has to investigate any attempt to grant a foreigner – any form of certificate – particularly a foreigner who has an order on his head – Mr Warner is under such an order. To announce plans to marry at this late date appears very odd indeed.

EDNA: Plans are nothing to do with you. They are my plans and Meadowlark's. I've never met you, I've never even heard of you and why don't you get off my back.

RAYMOND [*stiffly*]: Under CIA Act 62. I'll require a search of your documents and general baggage. And a search of your person to ascertain what I have to know.

EDNA: I demand to see Meadowlark now.

RAYMOND [*to* GERRY]: Mr Radinski will you go now and tell Mr Warner that the lady is here. And arrangements will be made in the near future for them. But Miss Walter must abide by regulations. I'll also require you to find a female police officer to take the search of person and possessions.

GERRY [*to* RAYMOND]: Blimey, you do make life difficult for yourself, you know.

[GERRY *leaves.* EDNA *takes a deep breath. She waits for the door to close.*]

EDNA: Creep!

RAYMOND: Nice coincidence isn't it? The very day you arrive the wedding banns are cleared! You can do better than that Miss Walter.

EDNA: It's Meadowlark's way. It's typical of him. He obviously planned it all as a big surprise and I was going to be whisked off the plane straight to the chapel wherever it was. Meadowlark's a romantic.

RAYMOND: I'll unromanticize the situation for you. If I have as much as a sniff of a suspicion you are in this to supply him with patrial status I'll book you under obstruction of justice, and conspiracy to defraud the Immigration Authorities.

EDNA: Brother are you twisted up in the head?

RAYMOND: Will you follow me please.

[LIGHTS.]

[*In the stage right office* MEADOWLARK *sits waiting. There are a number of chairs and tables. Piles of magazines and loose ashtrays. Zone of patience and detritus and the painful clock.*

GERRY *enters, sits down and starts to type with one finger.*]

MEADOWLARK [*despondent*]: . . . Where me woman, Blue Nose?

GERRY: She's arrived.

MEADOWLARK [*brightening*]: Tole yeh it was goin be meh great day.

GERRY: Raymond's giving her a rough ride.

MEADOWLARK: Edna too smart for him kindating.

GERRY: It's not all roses and champagne, mate.

MEADOWLARK: What do yeh care either way . . . ?

GERRY: I'm on your side. I'm likely to miss a football match to see you through this afternoon. I've sacrificed, laddie.

MEADOWLARK: Noffin that Raymond fellah can do to alter Edna once she medd up her mind.

GERRY: I wouldn't put too much weight on that one. Raymond's very persuasive in his own way. Edna's not going to find it easy. In fact, because of your crummy little problem, she's going through the ropes right now. All baggage strip. All clothes searched. And nice lady copper in the dressing-room for a quick body feel all round just for starters. How's that grab you, fucker? Off the record, that is.

[*The lights come on in the glass-panelled office stage left. Behind the frosted glass* EDNA *begins to disrobe; as she removes each item of clothing a female immigration officer checks it.*]

MEADOWLARK: Talkin bull, man.

GERRY [*fishing out a small booklet*]: Oh, yeah? 'Power to require a medical examination, Alien Conspiracy regulations, Clause so and so'.

MEADOWLARK: En no grounds no place to do that.

GERRY: '1. Require suspect disrobe before duty officer. 2. Remove clothes for separate inspection. 3. Require suspect open mouth. 4. Require suspect undergo hair and ear observation. 5. Duty officer to wear twelve-inch-length rubber gloves (hygiene washed). 6. Require suspect to lie on back for vaginal observation. 7. Require suspect to bend down for anal observation. 8. Provide suspect with dressing-gown during clothes inspection.

[MEADOWLARK *picks up a chair and brings it down towards* GERRY's *head.* GERRY *punches* MEADOWLARK *who subsides on to the floor.*]

Don't be stupid! You want the Law proper come down here give you right sorting over? I ain't trying to spit on you. I'm pointing out just what powers we got. You in real trouble, mate. One bad move from you, one lie from your girl – both out! Back to bloody where you come from. Just watch it. Just don't stretch it an inch OK . . . ?

[*As he backs away to the door. He opens the door and pauses.*]

MEADOWLARK: . . . Yeh bring meh woman, hear!

GERRY: Suspect's inspection first.

[*He shuts the door smartly as* MEADOWLARK *makes a move towards him again. There is a click on the door. As* MEADOWLARK *tries it, it is obvious it cannot be opened from the inside.*]

GERRY'S VOICE: Official security. All doors in this block open from the outside.

[GERRY'*s footsteps.*

MEADOWLARK *prowls. He can hear the steps fade away. He tosses the pile of magazines against the wall. He kicks at a chair. He seizes a desk and upends it. He rips the drawers out. He pushes the typewriter to the floor.* MEADOWLARK *tears up the last file he can find. Papers everywhere. Pauses exhausted.*

GERRY *is watching him from the doorway.* GERRY *takes out a white resistance jacket.* MEADOWLARK *is resigned to avoid another fight.* GERRY *approaches him and* MEADOWLARK *sinks inwardly.* GERRY *puts the jacket on* MEADOWLARK. *Enter* RAYMOND.]

GERRY: . . . Yer finished then?

MEADOWLARK: . . .

GERRY: The redecorations like?

MEADOWLARK: . . .

GERRY: There yer go . . .

MEADOWLARK: . . .

RAYMOND: Somebody will have to pay for this damage.

GERRY: Won't they just . . . I can handle it . . . OK?

RAYMOND: Watch he doesn't bite.

[RAYMOND *leaves.*]

GERRY [*to* MEADOWLARK]: He's not no animal is he?

MEADOWLARK: Why don yer gag meh mout an manahacle meh ankles whilst yer doin yer thing?

GERRY: It wasn't my idea – this strait-jacket. It was his – Raymond. We don't use old-fashioned nut-house equipment on the port. Any monkey trouble and it's a monkey-wrench in the mouth and band-aid when you wake up. Don't you agree?

MEADOWLARK: What're yer goin to do to me?

GERRY: I've got to stick by the rules, mate.

MEADOWLARK: Yer goin to tar an feather meh an put meh on the telegraph pole?

GERRY: That's not in the rules.

MEADOWLARK: Oh it ain is it? Yer surprises I, kindating.

GERRY: Look . . . you and me understand each other. Fact is . . . I got a brother gone much the same way as you gone, straight up.

MEADOWLARK: I don trust yerh . . . yer settin me up.

GERRY: You not suppose to trust me. You're forgetting your own rules – I'm the Law ain I?

MEADOWLARK: . . . White rhas . . . mon. Rhasclatt!

GERRY: You big black baboon.

MEADOWLARK: You're an Babylon blue-nose beast Albino freak of the north.

GERRY: Here watch it Cocoa or I'll lock you up in a dark room and make you disappear.

MEADOWLARK: I'll swing behind your neck you old jenarl you!

GERRY: Here what you going to do for a face when King Kong wants his arse back.

[MEADOWLARK *pauses. His only way of getting to* EDNA *is to laugh* GERRY *along. He laughs.*]

MEADOWLARK: You tinkin.

GERRY: I'm tinkin.

MEADOWLARK: I'm not laughin, me gums hurt.

GERRY: Is that right.

MEADOWLARK: Here Gerry, let me see my woman.

GERRY: No way Cocoa, that's way out of order.

MEADOWLARK: Oh please man. That Raymond fella givin her a rough time.

GERRY: All right then a quick two minutes.

[*They exit.*]

EDNA: Meadowlark.

MEADOWLARK: Show me your passport darlin.

EDNA: What! The man's got it.

MEADOWLARK: It blue?

46

EDNA: Yes.

MEADOWLARK: Yeh got work permit init?

EDNA: Yes.

MEADOWLARK: An all dem dates an stamps correct you know?

EDNA: Yes.

MEADOWLARK: A love yerh, Edna.

EDNA: Dad said you're a bad insurance risk.

MEADOWLARK: En got nah insurance.

EDNA: Do you know what I've just been through in the medical room! They said they wanted all my clothes to check for contraband. Then they said they wanted a body search for drugs. For God's sake tell me what you've done! And why have they put you in a strait-jacket?

MEADOWLARK: I in a bunch of trouble surrounded by a bunch ob white rats. Nuffin special bout dat. But dis is big trouble. They tryin to throw me outa the country just because something a little wrong with he papers, darlin, an dis was goin ter be the grettest day of meh life.

EDNA: Is it true? You've arranged a wedding?

MEADOWLARK: Swear to God, girl, it was all done an straightened out, and a would have met yeh off the plane an tekken yeh straight on down to the priestman. An we would have been wed before de jet-lag set in kindating. Best start de honeymoon with the least jet-lag so thought it best tekk yeh by surprise.

EDNA: But Meadowlark what exactly is going to happen?

MEADOWLARK: They wanna have me deported on the three o'clock plane to Jamaica.

EDNA: What!

MEADOWLARK: Am not goin teh Jamaica, am British thru an thru. A not running outa meh way to meet all them Jamaicans in Jamaica, meet enough Jamaicans right here in me front door don't I?

EDNA: What can you do about it?

MEADOWLARK: The priestman comin here to Gatwick Airport for the wedding kindating.

EDNA: Here!

MEADOWLARK: An he can do the wedding all nice right in dis building before the plane take off.

EDNA: Meadowlark, I'm scared.

MEADOWLARK: Edna you gotta go through with it, or I've had it. They'll sen me on dat plane, and they'll tink of something to arrest yeh for. I gotta big problem.

EDNA: All right Meadowlark, I'll do it.

MEADOWLARK: Yeh love me say tat – ?

EDNA: Yes.

MEADOWLARK: That ain't the problem.

EDNA: What is?

MEADOWLARK: De only ting harbouring on meh mind cenn yer oblige me with a loan fer?

EDNA: How much?

MEADOWLARK: £9·25 for the wedding certificate. No am not exactly broke a bin astute an left me spare change in a secret place that's all. Den I forget where the secret place is you know. It's meh head it's runnin off wit me body. Meh brain's on fire. Put your hands around my neck and give I a big wet kiss.

EDNA: Plenty of time for all that rum and coke.

MEADOWLARK: I'll never forget yeh Edna for dis.

EDNA: Why? Where you think you're going?

MEADOWLARK: Not going no place – just tinkin out loud.

EDNA: You'll find it difficult to forget me after all this because I'm not going to let you out of my sight for one minute.

MEADOWLARK: A know darlin.

EDNA: By coming here today, Meadowlark, my father has disowned me.

MEADOWLARK: Let's not tokk bout yer farther.

EDNA: And I hope there's going to be a honeymoon?

MEADOWLARK: Me too, mon.

EDNA: It's for ever and ever, Meadowlark?

MEADOWLARK: How long is dat?

EDNA: Against my better judgement I fell in love with you. My father had to go away on business. He left me alone for a few days in that London hotel. And you came along. You moved into the hotel if I remember right. You had some nerve.

MEADOWLARK: I wined yer an dined yer.

EDNA: An put it on my father's bill. And when Daddy came back he insulted you in front of me. But it was too late, I was in love.

MEADOWLARK: Me too, mon.

GERRY [*in door*]: Two minutes!

MEADOWLARK: Es all right. Everting come a go right. Yer don't worry. I love yer.

[RAYMOND *enters with* ELLIOT BRUCKNELL.]

RAYMOND: Will you come this way Mr Brucknell. Mr Warner is in here. Mr Brucknell, this is Miss Walter.

BRUCKNELL: How do you do.

EDNA: Hullo.

[GERRY *holds out his hand*.]

RAYMOND: And –

GERRY: How do you do, Vicar.

BRUCKNELL: You are Mr Warner?

GERRY: I'm Mr Radinski. This is Mr Warner for you, Vicar.

BRUCKNELL [*amazed*]: Mr M. Warner?

MEADOWLARK: Dat's I man name, sir, Priestman.

[BRUCKNELL *looks very confused*.]

BRUCKNELL: Mr M. R. Warner.

MEADOWLARK: A know we never met before, but meh time's not me own a heff so much on meh plate, yer see. Dat's why a couldn't come see you in first place.

[BRUCKNELL *takes off his homburg. He wears the traditional satin black skullcap, the 'yarmulkah'.*

BRUCKNELL *takes a deep breath*.]

BRUCKNELL: . . . Mr Warner? You are aware of the fact that I am a rabbi? And a minister of the Progressive Liberal Jewish Synagogue, Brixton?

GERRY [*eyes to ceiling*]: Hallo trouble . . .!

[RAYMOND *glumly tosses his files into the air*.]

ACT TWO

[RAYMOND *and* GERRY *are seated stage left in the large room.* MEADOWLARK *and* EDNA *sit centre.* BRUCKNELL *is seated stage right.*]

BRUCKNELL: Can we establish Mr Warner that you haven't been married before.

MEADOWLARK: No sir, Priestman.

BRUCKNELL: And you, Miss Walter.

EDNA: No, Rabbi.

BRUCKNELL: What is your first name Mr – ?

MEADOWLARK: Meadowlark.

BRUCKNELL: Ah . . . eh . . . Meadowlark.

MEADOWLARK: Am old Jamaican Jewish name.

BRUCKNELL: Meadowlark – why did you not come to me in the first place? Face to face?

MEADOWLARK: A was scerred. Yer sees me lekk dis all black an all what yeh tink? Some crazed black creppin in de door lock de door see. So a intended to come but on second thoughts sendin it roun in the post and done the banns at de Town Hall.

BRUCKNELL: You were afraid to come and see me because of your colour?

MEADOWLARK: Am a shy man.

BRUCKNELL: Well. It's understandable. But, it isn't my duty to provide anybody with a marriage service –

MEADOWLARK: En every body.

RAYMOND: He is not a member of the Jewish Faith. He is not a member of the Jewish Faith.

GERRY [*to* RAYMOND]: That's that then! I think I'll just about make the match this afternoon.

MEADOWLARK: En boastin but I a Jew. Moses yeh hear em say is black. Moses is a Jew.

GERRY [*to* RAYMOND]: Eh what time is Moses' plane did you say?

RAYMOND [*coldly*]: Ten to three. I'm going to confirm that booking now.

BRUCKNELL [*holds hand up towards* RAYMOND]:
   [RAYMOND *pauses.*]
   Just a moment Mr Borrall. Now Meadowlark, what are you trying to say?

EDNA: If he says he's a Jew he's a Jew! Isn't that enough, Rabbi?

BRUCKNELL: You say you are a Jew?

MEADOWLARK: Dat's what a say and I stickin.

GERRY: Sticking? You're coming apart at the seams.

BRUCKNELL: May I ask what services you have attended, Meadowlark?

RAYMOND: Yes, I'd like to know that.

MEADOWLARK: Never bin much inside de Brixton Synagogue. Bine dere once fer a cleanin job – didn't get dat neither. Bin often in Trenchtown wid me mother. Trenchtown, Jamaica.

BRUCKNELL: Which synagogue?

RAYMOND: Yes, which synagogue?

MEADOWLARK: Trenchtown Liberal Temple of Nimrod and de Holy Black Redeemer.

BRUCKNELL: I don't think I know it.

RAYMOND: Of course you don't know it. It doesn't exist. It doesn't exist.

BRUCKNELL: May I decide on that Mr Borrall.

GERRY: Our records say on your own evidence, you went to Jamaica with your dead father's passport.

RAYMOND: That's right. That's right. That's another lie.

MEADOWLARK: En no lie. A says a travelled with me ole man's passport after him dead. Am talkin about when I is a kid see.

GERRY: And how did you get to Jamaica in them days – on your waterwings?

MEADOWLARK: Meh muther married a Muslim after she divorced meh ole man, but she often come back to tekk me home. Her name is Rachel. Meh second first name is Rachel, right? She was born a Jew right? She want meh to follow de family tradition a tekk me to the Temple of Nimrod.

RAYMOND: Your mother took you back to Jamaica? How often? And how? And why did you not give me this information in your statement?

MEADOWLARK: She put meh face in her own Jamaican passport an fetch meh back an forth just when she lekk. When a was a kid. And yeh never asked meh for dis news when yer is interrogating teh shit out of meh. Sorry Rabbi.

BRUCKNELL: What did you do in this Temple of Nimrod?

MEADOWLARK: Had mehself de bar mitzvah. Bin through the circumcision bit. An read de books of de Lord.

RAYMOND [to himself]: Claims returned to Jamaica frequently on a Jamaican passport in the possession of his Jewish mother, who is now married to a Muslim.

[He turns back to MEADOWLARK.]

Once you were on your mother's passport I assume you never applied for Jamaican citizenship?

MEADOWLARK: No a didn't.

RAYMOND: On what grounds?

MEADOWLARK: A en Jamaican. Am Bridish tru and tru. Lived all meh life here give an tekk.

[Degree of cold despair on RAYMOND's face.]

BRUCKNELL: In this Temple of Nimrod, you studied what?

MEADOWLARK: All dem books.

BRUCKNELL: What books?

MEADOWLARK: Lissened to de readins. Spekk with priestman dere, an sing de Psalms of David. An diggin David most of teh time on account he never did much harm to teh ancient black world.

BRUCKNELL: What books, Meadowlark?

RAYMOND: Yes, what books?

MEADOWLARK: Firs am readin Torah book tekkin a peek at the Talmud an tinkin long lines of teh Ten Commandments kindating. Moses is a black mon.

BRUCKNELL: Have you studied the Pentateuch?

MEADOWLARK: Always done meh readin on de firs six books of de Ole Tessament.

BRUCKNELL: There are five books in the Pentateuch.

MEADOWLARK: Black Temple of Nimrod got dis sixth book made special tell black lekk us how to liff in whitey worl – Book of Nimrod.

BRUCKNELL: Never heard of it.

MEADOWLARK: Sure yeh ain. Is fer black peoples, not fer whites lekk yoursel.

RAYMOND: When is Passover?

MEADOWLARK: Third week am in March, right?

BRUCKNELL: Very good. And Hanukkah?

MEADOWLARK: December.

BRUCKNELL: The date of the New Year just past?

MEADOWLARK: Am not rememberin dat well, mebbe teh 22nd September mebbe am little bit after give an tekk coupla days.

BRUCKNELL: And what does Irene have to say about this?

EDNA: Who?

BRUCKNELL: You are Irene Edna correct?

EDNA: I'm Edna. There is no Irene in my name.

MEADOWLARK: Sometimes lekk see am callin her Irene a always call girls Irene sometimes its lekk calling them darlin, that's all.

EDNA: Never heard you call me Irene before!

MEADOWLARK: Well eff yer kindly shudup am callin yer Irene just for ole times sake!

EDNA [to BRUCKNELL]: The name is Edna, Rabbi.

BRUCKNELL: How's your knowledge of history, Meadowlark?

MEADOWLARK: Am doin meh best keep in touch with what happen yesterday yer know.

BRUCKNELL: Ancient history? Genesis remember? Solomon? Isaiah?

MEADOWLARK: En tinkin too much bout Solomon an Isaiah. All dat white history. Dere's Noah.

RAYMOND: Yes, there is Noah!

MEADOWLARK: Noah got his sons Shem and Ham. An Ham see his dad nekked an heff a giggle an Shem cover de old sod

53

up lekk, an Noah wake an kick poor old Ham outa de country. There's always people kickin other people outa the country!

[RAYMOND *pales.*]

An Ham runnin fetchit quick get his ass off teh hot seat, an all of a sudden he turn black old coal black mon he turn! Next minute Ham is father and Lord of Canaan, an all his sons black, and he got his son Cusit doin somting mekkin Carthage an nother son buildin Nineveh an great black Nimrod teh hunter fella knockin up tower of Babel in teh desert, all of em shit black yer know. An comin new times there's Solomon stealin all black kids for slaves for his temple –

BRUCKNELL: Very interesting.

MEADOWLARK: An tis idiot Joshua comin down an murderin all teh black Hamites livin in Canaan –

BRUCKNELL: Very very interesting.

MEADOWLARK: Next minute Babylon an Babel all destroyed, an the black tribes headin south to Ethiopia, an then Romans killin them all, then de Arabs slavin and lootin, then terh Turks doin it, then teh Portuguese then teh English whiteys shippin wholesale niggerloads mon by boat, stealin an lootin an ruining teh ancient black sons of dis guy Ham him seein Noah nekked, an a been cursed.

[*Stony silence. They stare at* MEADOWLARK.]

MEADOWLARK: Is teh true gospel of teh Liberal Jewish Temple of Nimrod.

[GERRY *and* RAYMOND *watch* MEADOWLARK *in disbelief.*]

BRUCKNELL: And so you have become a scholar of the Talmudic Faith, Mr Warner.

MEADOWLARK: En no scholar, am just a black Joo. Black soul spirit of de lost tribe, mon, seekin his rightful homelan an birthright in number 397 Coldharbour Lane, Brixton, SW 9, kindating.

RAYMOND: Have you quite finished?

MEADOWLARK: A guess.

RAYMOND: And so have I, I can tell you! [*looking up*] I am assuming you are an intelligent person, Miss Walter. The implausibility of this wedding must have sunk in to you. I intend to confirm the flight booking in order to carry out my warrant of deportation. And if I have any trouble with you whatsoever, I will press charges against you. Based on conspiracy to defraud the Immigration Appeal Tribunal findings, and based on common obstruction of the law.

EDNA: I hope you're not anti-semitic, Mr Borrall.

RAYMOND: Even if this wedding took place at the eleventh hour, you might still be liable for prosecution for aiding and abetting a proven absconded alien.

EDNA: I doubt that.

RAYMOND: Gerry!

[He exits.]

GERRY: Right you, out. [To MEADOWLARK] Shalom Cocoa. [GERRY and EDNA exit.]

MEADOWLARK: Mister Brucknell, sir, in fifteen minutes day are goin put meh on teh plane to Jamaica. Meh an Edna are en love. She come all dis way to live wit meh. All her papers are in order. An a could be naturalized just by this weddin business ting. I badly need help. I bin bad. I sinned you know. But would all dis happen eff meh colour was defferent? You a Joo en you? Yeh a alien too. Yeh got a blue passport?

BRUCKNELL: Yes.

MEADOWLARK: . . . Tekk yersel Priesman sir . . . before yer born en teh Babylon worl, yer ol mon heff a tredd dat troo?

BRUCKNELL: My father was a bespoke cutter.

MEADOWLARK: It makes sense don't it, tere's yer father cutting ef ter clot lekk, am got his tredd learn tere, right? Anyone wit any brainsmatter in ter working classes get his tredd in Babylon fixen up lekk. Yet look at meh, Priesman sir . . .

BRUCKNELL: I'm looking, Meadowlark.

MEADOWLARK: A cenn sew an a cenn knit, mon, see here – tese woolly tops. Do meh pearlie and do meh plainie tekk ter top of ter woollie an stitch me lekk here. An snip off ter curlie top for ter bobble ting stick-up lekk. See?

BRUCKNELL: So you like to call this your trade then?

MEADOWLARK: An I stitchin ter colours for Babylon oorope,

mon. Ter German krauts, mon. Ter French frogs. I working for the export drive. An I seekin a rightful place in meh troo home of origin kindating. Tell me tis, mon – ?

BRUCKNELL: Yes?

MEADOWLARK: Yer ole man got his tredd. An now yer got yer tredd. Yer burying em, giving birth ter em, yer doing yer prayers an laying out ter odds on ter Lord kinda . . . even yer marryin em off – too by too cordin to Moses, Priest-man.

BRUCKNELL: If you want to put it that way – yes.

MEADOWLARK: . . . Well, tis es ter tredd am doin, mon. Listen to me Priestman.

BRUCKNELL: I'm listening, Meadowlark.

MEADOWLARK: In de old days it was de Joos now it's de 'wogs'. Tis is meh own lan a'rm standin on.

BRUCKNELL: Meadowlark – I'm hardly convinced by your Temple of Nimrod and the Holy Black Redeemer, Trench-town.

MEADOWLARK: Don't blame teh Temple, blame me, I a bad Joo.

BRUCKNELL: That's beside the point.

MEADOWLARK: I a bad rarsin fella, I a bad character en doin any work spendin all meh time lying out on de pavement lekk them West Indian bums. Nuffin wrong wit bums. Trouble es no one will give us ter time ob der day.

BRUCKNELL: I'll ask you this – is there any binding oath you are prepared to stand by?

MEADOWLARK: Sure, Priestman. Name it.

BRUCKNELL: Are you in your heart being true to yourself?

MEADOWLARK: Is I.

BRUCKNELL: Is Edna of any Faith?

MEADOWLARK: No, Edna'll go long wiff I say-so.

BRUCKNELL: In other words she is a proselyte?

MEADOWLARK: En no pross nuffin, Edna's a good girl. Her's stickin wiv meh. Yeh goin wed we off? Sir, please.

BRUCKNELL: I have to say Meadowlark I must study, I must deliberate and I must consult.

56

MEADOWLARK: Or you're going to shit on I like the rest.

BRUCKNELL: And right now I have to make a phone call.

[LIGHTS UP *on stage right office.*

RAYMOND *enters followed by* GERRY.]

RAYMOND [*into phone*]: Caribbean Airways booking clerk, please.

GERRY: ... Hang about will you!

RAYMOND: Look, we only have a few minutes to pack him off on that plane. Yes, I'll hold on.

GERRY: This is not really going by the book, is it Raymond? You're exercising your own discretion to an alarming extent. I mean this is a grey area, Ray.

RAYMOND: Every time I want to believe something about this miserable man, he tops it with another absurdity. He says he's this, he's not. He does that, then he doesn't. He's marrying this person, all of a sudden he isn't. First his wife is Irish, next his wife is Guyanese. All of a sudden he is a Hebrew.

GERRY: Do you know what I think Ray and you're not going to like this. The one thing what gets under your skin is his colour.

RAYMOND: Rubbish.

GERRY: Otherwise, it's none of our business what girl will have him. Secretly, ever so secretly, it's deep inside you, mate, but you won't say it. And that's why you get all wound up inside. Look at me. All the time I was on the Port Authority – I never called a Chinese anything but 'chinky' and 'mustard'. During the war my eldest brother called them 'slant eyes' in Hong Kong. When you call one of these little fellahs 'mustard' you know where you stand and they know where they stand. You don't think about colour.

RAYMOND [*pause*]: ... You'll ... miss your football match.

GERRY: Give us a smile, Ray.

[RAYMOND *slowly creases up a wintry smile.*

GERRY *takes the phone from* RAYMOND.]

All right you asked for it ... Here you are – 14·50 hours. Caribbean Airways. One tourist class single c/o the Home Secretary's kitty-box.

[RAYMOND *snatches the phone from* GERRY]

RAYMOND: I . . . am not an unjust man.

GERRY [*pause. Silence.*]: . . . Tell you what, Ray, I'll have a little bet with you. If that rabbi walks in this door and says he'll underwrite the ceremony –

RAYMOND: I told you. I don't gamble.

GERRY: If he did say –

RAYMOND: Impossible.

GERRY: Ah, but if he did I'd let all the rest go by the board, and stand witness to the wedding, like I said before.

RAYMOND: And I'll lay you 100–1 against that rabbi stepping in here and saying the wedding's on.

GERRY: Done.

RAYMOND: Done.

[*There is a knock on the door.* GERRY *opens up. The* RABBI *steps inside.* RAYMOND *comes to his feet.* GERRY *and* RAYMOND *stare curiously at the* RABBI.]

BRUCKNELL: What time did you say Mr Warner's plane was supposed to leave.

[LIGHTS]

TANNOY [*V.O.*]: This is a final call for passengers flying Flight No. 6105, Caribbean Airways, 14·50 hours to Montego Bay, Jamaica. Will passengers please embark through gate nine. Thank you.

In the main area.

[*It is later.* GERRY *and* RAYMOND. EDNA *and* MEADOWLARK *hand in hand. The* RABBI *wears a white yarmulkah.*]

BRUCKNELL: Will the witnesses kindly step forward?

[GERRY *and* RAYMOND *sheepishly stand forth.*]

Rabbinic law requires that there shall be two witnesses in a marriage service. Further these two must be morally responsible persons. I shall quote you the law in Exodus (23: 1), 'You shall not join hands with an evildoer to give malicious evidence.' It is my duty to ask you the following questions. Have you, Raymond Arthur Borrall, knowingly indulged in usury?

RAYMOND: No.

BRUCKNELL: Have you, Raymond, knowingly indulged in gambling when it has been legally forbidden?

RAYMOND: No.

BRUCKNELL: Have you, Gerald Brod Radinski, knowingly indulged in usury?

GERRY: No, sir.

BRUCKNELL: Have you, Gerald, knowingly indulged in gambling when it has been legally forbidden?

GERRY: Eh . . . no, sir.

BRUCKNELL: Have either of you joined hands with an evildoer to make false testimony and malicious evidence against this couple.

RAYMOND:
GERRY: } No, sir.

BRUCKNELL: According to the rules of New Progressive Judaism, you are hereby installed as witnesses to Meadowlark Rachel's marriage to Irene.

EDNA: Edna, Rabbi.

BRUCKNELL: Yes. If anyone here present in the congregation has an objection, or claims thereby an impediment, in the marriage of these two people, let him speak forth now·

[MEADOWLARK *scrutinizes* RAYMOND. RAYMOND *slowly lowers his head. His feet shuffle.*

BRUCKNELL *gestures to* MEADOWLARK *and* EDNA *to step forward.*]

I am empowered, according to the Marriage Act (amended 1939), to supply you with a certificate of marriage in English law, under the auspices of the New Liberal Progressive Synagogue. Have you got the ring?

MEADOWLARK: Is in he pocket but a cannot quite reach it eff yeh see.

[*He shakes his handcuffs.*]

BRUCKNELL: Mr Radinski, would you like to remove those handcuffs?

GERRY: Oh certainly, Rabbi.

[GERRY *does so with a key.*

BRUCKNELL *opens his case, and pulls out a cassette. It plays holy music.*]

BRUCKNELL It is customary for the bridegroom to lay on a feast for his bride's family. I suppose that in this case –

[*He opens it and takes out a bottle of red wine and two glasses.*]

MEADOWLARK: Feast? Don't worry none bout any feast, mon, a'll be heffin a good time with Edna in teh Jamaica patti shop all night long and they havin a licence too, down by Brixton Market.

EDNA: What happened to the caviar and the champagne buffet, Meadowlark?

MEADOWLARK: Effin an blindin ole hell a must heff let it slip meh mind.

BRUCKNELL [*fetching the bottle forward*]: I assumed you'd need a drink to toast to the couple, and so I took the liberty of bringing a bottle of Ruby sherry.

MEADOWLARK: How much dat goin set I back, sir?

BRUCKNELL: Cheapest Ruby type wine. SouthAfrican – £1·95 with VAT. Very sweet.

[BRUCKNELL *prepares a white and blue satin canopy. It has poles at either end. He hands either end each to* GERRY *and* RAYMOND. *They hold it up like an oblong umbrella.*]

Will the witnesses please hold this canopy. This chuppah is the ancient pavilion under which the original nuptials were consummated. Are we all ready?

[RAYMOND *glances at his watch nervously.* MEADOWLARK *sees him.*]

MEADOWLARK: What time yeh got dere, Raymond, sir?

RAYMOND [*eyes raised*]: Exactly a quarter to three.

GERRY: Bang goes my football match.

RAYMOND: I think Walthamstow Wanderers can do without a reserve goalkeeper, Mr Radinski.

MEADOWLARK: Dis two horse race on, Mister Rabbi, sir?

BRUCKNELL: The witnesses will be required to wear something on their heads.

MEADOWLARK: Ah can fix that.

[MEADOWLARK *thinks quickly. He snaps his fingers. He*

opens his polythene bag of woolly tops and picks out one for
RAYMOND. MEADOWLARK *puts it on* RAYMOND'*s head*.]

MEADOWLARK: How's that?

RAYMOND [*stiffly*]: . . . Thank you.

[MEADOWLARK *puts it down low over* RAYMOND'*s brow
and ears as if he'd like to hide behind it. He stares balefully
out. The sides are low over his ears and make them jut out.*]

MEADOWLARK [*with* GERRY'*s woolly*]: It teh special Arsenal
colours just for you, Gerry.

[MEADOWLARK *puts the woolly on* GERRY. BRUCKNELL
gestures to MEADOWLARK *and* EDNA *to stand together. He
shuffles* GERRY *and* RAYMOND *holding up the chuppah into
position. Above the couple's heads.*]

BRUCKNELL: Blessed be you who come in the name of the Lord;
we bless you from the house of the Lord. The congregation
will sit.

[GERRY *and* RAYMOND *sit on chairs holding up the chuppah.*]
Do you take this woman to be your wife, promising to honour
and to love her, to sustain her and to keep her and to be unto
her a faithful husband?

MEADOWLARK: A does.

BRUCKNELL: Do you take this man to be your husband, promising to love and to honour him, ever to seek his welfare and
to be unto him a faithful wife?

EDNA: I do, Rabbi.

BRUCKNELL: He who is supreme in majesty, beyond all praise
and infinitely great, may He bless the bridegroom and the
bride.

[*He gestures to* MEADOWLARK *to give him the ring.* MEAD-
OWLARK *produces it after a struggle in his pockets.*]

BRUCKNELL [*holds up ring*]: This ring is the seal of the bond
which shall bind you together as husband and wife. May it
keep you ever mindful of your solemn promise to be loyal to
one another, and to establish a true household in Israel, dedi-
cated to God and filled with His presence. The congregation
will stand.

[GERRY *and* RAYMOND *climb to their feet.*]

We praise You, O Lord, our God, King of the Universe, by whose laws Jewish marriage is sanctified. The bridegroom places the ring on the bride's finger and says to her after me –

[*As he hands the ring back to* MEADOWLARK *and* MEADOWLARK *pops it on* EDNA'S *finger.*]

By this ring you are betrothed to me according to the Law of Moses and Israel.

MEADOWLARK: By tis ring yeh is betrothed teh I accordin to teh Law of Moses an Israel.

EDNA [*to* MEADOWLARK]: By this ring you are betrothed to me according to the Law of Moses and Israel.

BRUCKNELL: The congregation will sit.

[BRUCKNELL *takes out a cassette tape from his case. The music is Rabbinical Liturgy i.e. ceremonial.* GERRY *and* RAYMOND *sit.*]

Even as your love will enhance the sweetness of joys, so will it lighten life's burdens. For henceforth you will share all things.

[*He glances at* GERRY *and* RAYMOND.]

The congregation will stand and say 'Amen' after me. We praise You, O Lord our God, King of the Universe, Creator of the fruit of the vine.

GERRY: ⎫
RAYMOND: ⎬ Amen.

BRUCKNELL: We praise You, O Lord our God, King of the Universe, who has given us life, sustained us and brought us to this happy day.

GERRY: ⎫
RAYMOND: ⎬ Amen.

BRUCKNELL: We praise You, O Lord our God, King of the Universe who have created all things for Your Glory.

GERRY: ⎫
RAYMOND: ⎬ Amen.

BRUCKNELL: We praise You, O Lord our God, King of the Universe. . .

RAYMOND: [*jumps gun*]: Amen!

BRUCKNELL: Creator of man.

GERRY:
RAYMOND: } Amen!

BRUCKNELL: We praise You, O Lord our God, King of the Universe who have made man in Your own image.

GERRY:
RAYMOND: } Amen.

BRUCKNELL: Grant abundant happiness to these Your children united in love. Fill them with that joy which, according to the ancient legend, Your children experienced in the Garden of Eden. We praise You, O Lord, who cause the bridegroom and bride to rejoice.

GERRY:
RAYMOND: } Amen.

BRUCKNELL: Speedily let there be heard in the streets of Jerusalem, happiness and exultation, gladness and brotherhood, peace and friendship. And in all the world.

[MEADOWLARK *glances at* GERRY *and* RAYMOND. GERRY *beams.* RAYMOND *wriggles.*]

The congregation will sit.

[BRUCKNELL *takes a glass from the case. Wraps it in a white cloth. Places it beneath* MEADOWLARK'S *foot.* MEADOWLARK *crushes it.*]

BRUCKNELL: Mazeltov!

MEADOWLARK: Musseltap!

[*Each time* GERRY *and* RAYMOND *sit and stand they have to wrestle with the chuppah pavilion in their hands.*]

I declare you both husband and wife. According with Jewish tradition. According with the laws of this country. I invoke God's blessing upon you both. The congregation will stand.

[GERRY *and* RAYMOND *struggle up again.*

The RABBI *fetches the wine and pours out two glasses.* EDNA *and* MEADOWLARK *share a glass. They kiss warmly. Then they both sip at the wine.*

In turn the RABBI *gives* GERRY *then* RAYMOND *a sip of wine from the spare glass. They are still holding up the chuppah.*

MEADOWLARK *and* EDNA *hug.* GERRY *steps forward and*

shakes MEADOWLARK's *hand. Followed by* RAYMOND *a little less effusive. They formally shake* EDNA's *hand.*]

GERRY: There you go then you great black Cocoa!

MEADOWLARK: Yer somffin off a great white Cocoa yoursel.

GERRY: You didn't mind me calling you a black bastard the odd time?

MEADOWLARK: Long as a can call yeh a white one.

GERRY: Ain't much difference is there?

MEADOWLARK: Cept yeh had more experience at it kindating.

RAYMOND: Congratulations – Mr Warner, and Mrs Warner.

EDNA: Thank you, Raymond.

RAYMOND [*to* MEADOWLARK]: There was just one final question I wanted to ask you but I just can't seem to bring it to mind –

MEADOWLARK: Yearh . . . an a tole I goah beat up Babylon an heff meh a great day didn't I? It's a great day, Mister Priestman, sir, mekkin no mistake. Cheers, mon!

[BRUCKNELL *takes out of his pocket a slip of paper which looks suspiciously like a bill. He hands it to* MEADOWLARK.]

BRUCKNELL: Including the wine, cost of the marriage certificate and my return bus fare home, that'll be £13·64 plus VAT, Mr Warner. Prompt payment gratefully received. No cheques thank you without banker's card. The Lord God is thy guide. Many congratulations to you both!

[LIGHTS]

Back in the Brixton room.

[*As* MEADOWLARK *helps* EDNA *with her suitcase. She looks around the room. The bright orange walls and green bedspread.*]

MEADOWLARK: Yer comin right in see teh wedding honeymoon suite mebbe needs fer a fast dustup do de honours lekk.

EDNA: So this is the two-roomed apartment with bathroom and balcony you wrote to me about in detail? And eh . . . I'm looking for the electric freezer combine fridge you talked about in your letter? Let's see – what was it? And a wall-door German oven with an infra-red ray cook-spit, Meadowlark.

MEADOWLARK: Es mebbe not the cream of the property market. It's the greatest day of my life. Come to bed.

EDNA: When did you last wash these filthy dishes?

MEADOWLARK: I'll mekk teh bed an push all tis rubbish unner de antique chest of drawers. En no fridge, too cole in England heff a fridge, makes whole place kinda fridge kindating. Spen extra money on freezin. But it's lovely and warm in the bed.

EDNA: Meadowlark – it's filthy in here! You've got mice an all! Look!

MEADOWLARK: Mon needs a touch of company kepp body an soul tickin together . . . Now I have you is much better. I'm ready for you, darlin!

EDNA: I'm awful tired, darlin. Been on that plane six hours and then the customs. Then those immigration people and filling the forms in.

MEADOWLARK: Tats whad a say. Tekk yeh clothes off an jump into bed.

EDNA: I'll get into bed but I don't want any fooling around with my body just this yet.

MEADOWLARK: Dat's what I say, just take your clothes off and git straight tween teh sheets an pretend old Meadowlark not here at all.

EDNA: Well turn the light off then.

MEADOWLARK: Ennyfing yer heart desire sure . . .
[*He turns the light off. In the blackout.*]

EDNA: The jet-lag is getting me and I'm cold.

MEADOWLARK: Ole jet-lag neffer heff effect on meh . . . Edna . . . you right?

EDNA [*yawning again*]: Yes I'm right.

MEADOWLARK: . . . Edna darling.
[*The lights come back on.*]

EDNA: . . . You really love me for ever, Meadowlark?

MEADOWLARK: Yes, darlin.

EDNA: . . . I don't know why I love you. Things you have put me through. And my father. And the money you cost me. It's all my savings.

MEADOWLARK: Darlin.

EDNA [*quite matter of fact*]: And you've got no job, no real prospects. You haven't even got a car.

MEADOWLARK: Edna.

EDNA: I don't much like your friends I met last year. This room is a rat-trap. And I suppose you think you're going to live off me. Where am I going to hang my clothes? Is there a decent shop in walking distance?

MEADOWLARK: Darlin.

EDNA: And how can I cook on a single ring connected to the gramophone plug socket? I'm hungry, Meadowlark.

MEADOWLARK: What!!

EDNA: You go and get some food and I'll wait for you all nice and warm in the bed.

MEADOWLARK: All right. Where's your purse, darlin?

EDNA: Under my clothes.

[*He finds her bag.*]

EDNA: Be quick, Meadowlark.

MEADOWLARK: All right, I'll be back in a split.

[*He exits to the Jamaican patti shop.*]

[*into the kiosk window.*] . . . A done chickens? An breadfruit chutney? Two tin uglifrut. Two poun weight green bananas. Two poun weight sweet potatoes. New World freezpack crayfish for two. An Jooish melons? No? Jamaican melons then. Packet semolina. Tin concentrated milk. Four large lemonades. Haff of Cap'n Davy rum. Almos forgot packet ganga peas an teh sweet peppers. Got yerself change of a tenner? What yer mean teh change en worth spit. From all this? Get goin, tekk the change round to de pub teh waitin killin meh guts. This is the grettest day of meh life yer know, so don't keep me on suspension.

[*While* MEADOWLARK *orders,* IRENE *enters in the darkness into* MEADOWLARK's *room. She sits on the bed and surprised lets out a scream.* EDNA *rises from the bed, wrapping a sheet around her. She fetches a glass of water from the sink-unit and brings it back to* IRENE.

The lights fade on the Jamaican patti shop and as MEADOW-LARK *returns to his room the lights rise there.*]

. . . Didn't dey feed yer nuffin board teh plane now? Darlin?
[*Sees* IRENE *and jumps out of his skin.*] . . . Who de fokk is
tis?

IRENE: [*bursts into tears*]: Aargh.

EDNA: She's called Irene!

MEADOWLARK: Neffer seen her before in meh –

EDNA: You proposed marriage to her at a quarter to seven this
morning in this room.

MEADOWLARK: What!

EDNA: And you jilted her at half-past twelve this morning in
the Immigration Office, Gatwick!

MEADOWLARK: A deny dat.

EDNA: You're an alltime low louse let-go beast shit!

MEADOWLARK: A deny dat.

EDNA: You're a shit.

IRENE: You're a shit.

MEADOWLARK: Yeh fokkin kepp out of dis Irene. Whoever
yeh is! Yeh don't know shit! A never seen yer in I life
before.

EDNA: Irene has lived with you here for week after week feeding
and loving you. You have treated her like dirt.

MEADOWLARK: A neffer laid hans on a woman since a last spend
that week wiv her in teh Jubilee Festival kindating! When yeh
father met me.

EDNA: And you'd have been on a plane to Ireland with her, and
I'd have arrived and there was nobody here to meet me. My
father warned me all right! And you took advantage of me
because I was a virgin, and because you knew how much I
hated my family. And wanted to escape. You shit, you.

IRENE: Shit!

MEADOWLARK [*to* IRENE]: What de ras yer doin in tis room
screwin up I affairs! Tryin blackmail me fer money? En got
none.

EDNA: She came back here because her heart is broken. She
imagined you'd been sent back to Jamaica and she just wanted
to spend a last night in this bed, you shit you! Tell him Irene!
    [IRENE *starts to speak.*]

67

She came back because she had a key to return, and because she brings back these tickets for tonight for this dogs' race thing at . . . What is it?

IRENE: Catford.

EDNA: Catford. All out of her goodness, you shit you!

[*She waves the tickets at him and puts them on the table. She then pushes* MEADOWLARK *away from the table.*]

EDNA: Come on Irene! We might as well help prepare this green figs, and salt fish and yam slices. Jamaican rubbish!

[EDNA *tears apart a couple of cooked chickens. She finds knives and forks and slams them down noisily on the table. Bang! Bang!* IRENE *gets up courage and follows suit. She crashes tins of lemonade and cups on to the table. She roughly jerks the chairs around the table.* EDNA *industriously sorts out items of food for as quick a meal as she can make up.*]

. . . You are the worst damn good-for-nothing lazy shit man I've ever heard!

MEADOWLARK: En so easy now, en eight out of ten guys en got jobs, Edna!

EDNA: . . . You are the most lying cheating and dishonourable man who ever lived and was born on earth!

MEADOWLARK: Am trying to improve I image now.

EDNA: The most uneducated badass ignorant Trenchtown bum I've met. You belong in a tin shack ghetto eating nothing but rotted ganga peas and counting ticks on your nose!

IRENE: I'm glad he can hear somebody else say it for a change, Edna.

MEADOWLARK [*crouching*]: Oh Lord a got women trouble. Dey in league.

EDNA: You are the most brainless, unthinking and uncaring hyena on the face of it!

MEADOWLARK: What a done now?

EDNA: It's what you haven't done! You are the meanest cheat-ingest no hope 'nigger' I have seen today.

MEADOWLARK: A en all bad.

EDNA: The meanest cheatingest black Jew 'nigger' shit heard of!

MEADOWLARK: Am remindin yeh tis our wedding day honey-moon ting, Edna . . . Darlin?

EDNA: Every sin you'll suffer for. Every little mistake you've made. You will pay.

MEADOWLARK: Darlin. A can't believe yer talkin teh the mon you love. I'm just ole Meadowlark.

[IRENE *and* EDNA *tuck into the food.*]

EDNA: Come along, Irene. Never mind that heap of worthless shit lying there!

MEADOWLARK: Oh Lordie is I now, an am finding big trouble here.

IRENE [*to* EDNA]: It's a case of something about two fish in the sky better'n one bird in the sea, kindating. Ay Edna?

MEADOWLARK: How'd a find meself in tis fix of porridge, Lord?

EDNA [*to* IRENE]: Until he pulls his badass together he's going to have hell. Eat your chicken now Irene.

MEADOWLARK: I tinkin on resignin teh human race.

EDNA [*to* IRENE]: It was nice of you Irene to offer us those tickets for the-what-is-it? – the races at Catford tonight you bought. I'll be sure you get paid for them. Come all the way back here and out of your kindness offer them to me!

MEADOWLARK: An meh tinkin teh fixin it teh be the grettest day of meh life, you know!

EDNA [*to* MEADOWLARK]: You're going to be allowed to get away with nothing. And what is this. A filthy dustbin inside the room smelling the arse off me! You just put that outside the door in the hall this instant, please kindly. You're going to be nagged morning, noon and night.

[MEADOWLARK *takes the bin and starts to clear the scraps from the table. We see him neatly take the Catford tickets.*]

EDNA: You're going to be battered into shape. You're going never to have no peace until the cows come home. You'll get no sympathy. And you'll have nothing from me but the pointy end of my tongue. Want money you work! Want drink you don't bring it back in here! No doing it on credit! You'll stop gambling. You'll stop loving up every white woman in the street. You'll queue up at Social Security like everybody else. You'll dress nice. And you'll pay once a month for my dreadbeads at the hair stylist! And you'll be home on time for each meal I cook. On the dot of time.

[MEADOWLARK *exits*.]

Frankly, Meadowlark, you are in for one hell of a marriage with me you are. And hell it will be! Eat your sweet peppers, Irene! You hear me, Meadowlark? He's skulking now. You hear me?

IRENE: Meadowlark.

EDNA: Meadowlark!

IRENE [*glancing down*]: The Catford dog tickets!

EDNA:
IRENE: } Meadowlark!!

MEADOWLARK: Meadowlark!!!

[*Out of the shadows suddenly* RAYMOND *and* GERRY *jump forward. They almost lift* MEADOWLARK *off his feet.* RAYMOND *draws breath.*]

RAYMOND: Mr Warner there was just one final question I wanted to ask you.

[MEADOWLARK *stares at* RAYMOND. RAYMOND *hesitates, seemingly lost in a grey area.*]

RAYMOND: But I just can't quite bring it to mind. I . . .

[RAYMOND *and* GERRY *lower* MEADOWLARK *to the ground.* MEADOWLARK *pulls himself together.*]

MEADOWLARK: Eff yer carn remember teh question, man, forget I teh arnser.

[LIGHTS]

END

Full Frontal

Full Frontal was first presented at the Theatre Upstairs, London, on 13 February 1979.

Gabriel Nkoke WINSTON NTSHONA

Directed by Rufus Collins
Designed by Jim Clay

[*Two doors. One is heavy with reinforced wood flats and four-inch screws. The other is a half-glazed affair. A chair. A desk.*

GABRIEL *kind of easy. He slowly opens the heavy door. Slips in. Slips out back from us. Calling. Reaches the glazed door the screen away from us side. Taps. Holds. Slides in. Smiling ever so.*]

GABRIEL [*on the pavement*]: ... Knock, knock. Who this? Friend I say? ... [*Pushes door.*] ... Halloo ... [*Back of screen.*] ... [*Taps on glaze.*] ... That you in there man, sir? That you? [*Pokes head on stage round glaze.*] ... I'm Gabriel. You the man I come to see? Pleased to meet you.

[*Book misses his head by an inch.*]

... No. I ain't no cleaner. Door was open downstairs. No I ain't applying for the cleaning. That's right.

[*Book flies at him. Ducks back.*]

... Take it easy will you. I'm not from Social Security. I'm telling. And I'm not from the West Indian World man! Do I look like a West Indian for Christ's sake!

[*Book punches the wall beside him as he shows back from behind the door.*]

... I ain't West Indian man. Got dignity man. Don't confuse me now. I'm not jah roots Caribbean dreadlocks man. I'm just Gabriel man, how do you do man! Sir.

[*He catches the next book and steps forward and returns the book onto the desk.*]

... Yearh, I like books, too! What's this – *Civilized Man's Eight Deadly Sins* by Konrad Lorenz? 'Study of man's loss of contact with his environment'? I'll buy that one, sir. Yes, sir, mister ... What? ... No, sir, man, nobody sent me round from the Commission of Racial Equality as a practical joke. A few weeks back I filled in my membership application.

And I posted you my £3 membership fee in the post see. To here, sir, National Front HQ, Southall, sir. Here, sir. And then I ask myself why I been kept waiting so long for my membership card. And just now, I'm walking past your window and . . . no, sir, no, I'm not trying to make a monkey out of you! Not me. All right, sir. I'm not a monkey, either. Nor a baboon. No, nor a dog-faced Manchurian gorilla in rut, sir. No, sir, not wearing make-up. I'm the real me. A shade pink underneath the palm wine glow if you follow my thinking.

. . . Name is Gabriel, sir. Gabriel Nkoke, 47b Manasser Avenue, Garden entrance, Southall . . . Sir? I'm not in there, sir, in those files? . . . N-K-O-K-E – Nkoke. What? You've got a G. N. Koke? K-O-K-E? Well, obviously, that is a mistake somebody must have made here in the files, sir. I have no middle name beginning with the letter N. Name is Nkoke. I understand the misunderstanding. Anybody can make a mistake like that and I . . .

[*More books fly at him.*]

. . . A lying black layabout oddball freak? Me, sir? You mean one of them Trinidadians you mean. Too much Brylcream on their dreadlocks seeped into their minds. All that rasti Israelite crap, all that natti dread sufferation done their heads power of harm. Leroy Smart tropicalized Brown Sugar! Sir. They stole that from Africa, sir. They took it they did . . .

. . . I'm your new member man, sir. [*Ducking.*]

You'll do those books just no good at all. If you want to keep them nice and tidy.

. . . I don't want my money back. I'm not a Communist. I'm not a Trot. No, nobody set me up from the British League. I don't know no one from the British League. British League nothing but a bunch of fascist thugs I know that, man. Never heard of SWP, no. No, sir, don't have a union. No union sent me up here trick you down. I been a dock worker all this past year, but a little trouble the convenor tells me with my joining the union. Would I like to apply to Trans-

port and General Workers if I want to make a union? I say
I don't mind. But I think I don't care much for that union
no how.

... So while I am standing here, on the corner of the road,
and I happen by to see your door, I thought step right in
and say to the National Front man in his office, here I am
man, and do I get my membership card now?

... Huh? Well, I'm not arguing. I don't think you see my
way of seeing it, sir. I agree, I agree, I might look like a shit-
arse gollywog first time see me. But I'm not, sir. No, sir. I'm
not a commie nigger queer. No, sir. I don't carry clubs with
nail studs. Ssshh, sir. Sssh, sir, now. I'm on your side. Not
me. You mean one of them Trinidadians you mean. All that
rasti Israelites rubbish an de blood in de woods reggae nonsense. Not me, sir. All that natti dread sufferation done their
heads a power of harm. I'm African, sir. I got a country I'm
on way back to. I got *alusi* gods in the forest and Ibo masks
on my walls. I got black divination of *nsi* ghosts. All that
reggae crap? Black New York Zionists control all the record
shops in Jamaica, sir. Where'd that steel drumming come
from? Come from ancient *oja* music, man of the hairy moun-
tains legend, black West African *oja* sound ripped off by
street louts pick up a couple of cat's tail tin cans. I want see
every last West Indian, and reggae rasti Jamaican patti head
sent back where they belong, sir. Why do they like it here?
Because they don't like there? Why's that? Because they
ain't never had anything there in first place. They came from
Africa, and they lost that. Don't pay mind to that black tribe
of Ethiopia only thing they ever been doing they been the
lost tribe all right, they lost their tribal heads drinking rum
and cola. Now they won't drink that no more now white man
has found his white rum with his lemonade white blonde
with her peroxide tongue down the glass.

... Not talking racist hatred, sir. No. Talking racialism now
sir, National Front tells me that's still legal. Different
between us, right?

... Why I want to join the Front? I read the words on the

banner in the last march. I saw all those lefty louts tossing bricks. I saw all those white policemen push to the front of the fight only two token nigger cops they got. I sense the unease when I walk in a shop and they all turn round glance at me think to themselves, uh-huh here come another rastas black thief with a knife on his hip. I'm leaving sometime soon this year going back to Port Harcourt. I can't wait taste red lobster and ganga peas, drink it back down with palm fruit light and cola-nut crush come out the village freezer. In our village we had the boss chief keep the gàs fridge in his hut until one day we all asked where all this summer's cola crush vanished to? And the boss chief said, 'Oh that, that all it's about, I drank it.' If he'd drunk that much cola he'd been in hospital my father said. I remember the chief got stick from my father. And we found the money hidden under the hut in the earth. And my father said to him, 'Oh yes, that's where you drank it, you stole, you thief bastard chief' – and a few other choice Igbo demon threats about evil birds come down and peck his eyes and hairy trees catch the chief, never let him go – when my father took the place of the chief, he put a padlock on the fridge and hung the key round his neck. Then my father come a cola wine drinkard soft in the head because I never see the key round his neck. Old *ntwengo* tapper tapped his own head.

. . . What makes me think I'm a man for your party? I've seen the light. I've done all those things and I'm ashamed. I took a white wife. Janine, she was. I never so much as married her. But we had the good thing on. Like the yankees pretend they still in some ghetto. Good thing, mind you, come back to old brown sugar cheatin me dry, sir. Janine and I had a baby. Little Ralph. Cross colour of *sawa* fish and old *tete* laid out too much in the sun. And I was working so hard all the day long doing my clerking down on the docks and the union still saying, 'Oh not this union, try famous Mr Jack Jones union.' And Janine starts taking up with this Jamaican. Abdul Jerry. They still talking Muslim black *hajis*, find Mecca bottom of a reggae float drum, and this

76

Abdul Jerry come on all the same mouthwash. Yes sir, I say, I see you get away with my Janine behind my back like that. Jamaican flatfoot from Clapham North, like as have not he spent all his hardass labour squatting outside Social Security but you don't get away with it with me, I tell you. And I am coming home dogbeat in my bones and I catch him and Janine in my bed. Fight start up, Janine scream. And soon someone call the police and I say to the blue helmet man take these two to the jailhouse for infidelity, stealing a man's woman, using his bed without as much as a by-your-leave, and doing it all indecent and all in front of young Ralphie in his cot. I'm left with just the baby in my arms now and I don't see Janine so much anymore. I hear she's done her hair in voodoo plaits and acquired a 'genuine dreadbead wig'! It gets so low now, don't it? . . . I feel shame.

. . . How can you say that! I've got no respect? I must be out of my mind to think I can join the Front? You've got it mistaken there, sir. I'm in full agreement. I support the Queen, I support a New Commonwealth Union of Canada, Australia and New Zealand and Great Britain. I reckon you should get this country out of the Common Market. There's three million – don't pay any attention to what those liberals say in the Commission of Racial Equality – at least three million Jamaicans, Afro-Asians in this lovely country, sir. You throw them all out. I'm African man, sir, and I've got a home on the west coast to go to. Rise in violence is black kids . . . I been mugged, man, outside my own door. Rise in unemployment is all black kids, they're unemployed in this culture. I got a good job, sir, and I got my own native village Ogwe life, north of Lagos. Rise in number of prisoners living off the state is all black youth got no sense of purpose but knife and lift pockets and rip off handbags. That's what I always did say, repatriate, nothing up front, not a penny, just the boat trip. This is a land of strangers. Shirkers and wastrels out. Is my car taxed? Yes, sir. Is the h.p. paid up? Yes, it is. Is the insurance comprehensive? Well, just about. I'm suspicious of my insurance company. Called Rothschild and Rothschild, Rothschild House, Enfield by-pass, opposite the new police dog-pound. But I say, like the Front says, sir, that the Jews is all past history. Isn't it true you have Jews on your membership list? How many? Two? Well, that's a start. If you can take a Jew, sir, man, you can give me my membership card, that's what I'm saying. Because I'm preaching just exactly what you're supporting. My opinion on capital punishment? Hang em, man, high! My position on the economy? I agree with what the National Front stand by. Too much loose money around the place. No bank to loan anymore than what they already have in their vaults. I know how much money there is. Maybe 800 million pound notes all over the place, and who got it? You have to take half of that, and put it aside, because that's all in the hands of the Jewish banks and the Lord himself don't know where they hide all that. Nobody else got much money. The landowner farmer got none. The man with a wage packet only see it in a brown envelope once a Friday evening. I give you a straight guess one whole quarter of all those millions going out the Post Office every week to Delhi and Trinidad, bet your brown sugar illusions it do.

... Who got the rest, sir? All the bookies are Jews. One. All the slot-machine owners are Irish. Two. All the gasmeter collections and all the car meters are run by the Chinese dragon mafia. Three. Where's the rest of the cash? It's in the bus conductors' bags, and it's in the underground ticket collection points, and we all know who runs that, sir, the entire rastas reggae Caribbean gangs got control of all that! I see your point. It's about time British money was returned to the British nation. Am I right, sir? You know how much the rastas gangs want for deposit to get become a bus conductor – £400 down in greens, man. And 20 per cent of the cut from the weekly leather bag. It's shocking ... Each time you give a Trinidad ticket man at the underground an extra 20p because you haven't paid your fare right at the other end, you're giving the country's money away.

... Me, sir, man? I've got a home to go to. I've got a job.

I've got a country home I'm going back to, pay my own fare. I got my own music and my dark hairy ghosties in the forest and plenty of the good stuff to drink, got my own food and my own women back in the village, and I've seen the writing on the white wall. Next thing come up this Charlie Prince of Wales marry a black girl from Georgetown and the entire nation of British aristocrats all take on suddenly the colour of Nescafé and there's not one white left at all in the United Kingdom cept for the Jews. Then you can see the white writing. Who profit most then, sir? Jews do the profiting. In no time, whole damn country find the only true whitey looking white is the Jewish mafia from Golders Green, and before you found the lockshen soup gone cold all the Jews got the entire crown jewels and sitting in the tower behind a wall of barbed wire. And the entire aristocracy banished to Aston, Birmingham, where they got nothing but Nescafé skins, and they can merge with the crowd.

... All Communists out. All black liberals put in jail. All white liberals lose their Social Security rights. And if I want free medical attention in the United Kingdom my government back in Lagos got to provide the reciprocal free attention to as many Britons. Repeal the Race Relations Act? Yes, sir. Repeal the British Nationality Act of 1948? Yes, sir, man. What is more inflationary than to pay one and half million unemployed? I agree with you. One and a half million men paid to do nothing but silly-arse sit until Social Security say com'n fetchit, boy; I won't buy that one.

... Don't think when I get back home, whole village isn't going to look at my son Ralph and declare 'Who this, Gabriel now?' Little light-skinned thing about to walk never seen a green banana tree in his life never learned play in an *ojo* mud-bed outside the hut and I tell them he learn. But they'll look away. Maybe I'll tell them about the £45 a week on the King George docks, clerking makeweight time for the Polish and Japanese ships. Then there's the two-bedroom flat on Southall High, and the council allow me extra £1.80 for Ralphie's supplemental diet now his mother no longer around. And the village turn round to me say, 'You just Ogwe material white waste man been dyed another shade lighter.' They'll smile when Ralphie grows up and ask for his Mother's Pride loaf, and all I'll find him is soft-bake cassava wrapped in bitter-leaf. He'll learn.

. . . What passport I possess? Brand new Nigerian passport. Beneath my rights take a British passport. You keep your and I'll keep my, that's what I say.

. . . No, sir, I don't hold with the word integration. Diseased minds of the Jews want to milk black Nescafé, want to hook us to death with their Chinese heroin, want to feed blacks with civil right rules O K. Bullshit it's a con. *Extigration*. That's my word.

. . . Let me ask you this – isn't it true the black country deserve its own? And the white its own, too? That's what the Front stand by, that so sir? Yes. When I read that the National Front sees all liberal rules O K as a mass con perpetrated by red and red street-fighters in order to soften up the capitalist process, I understood then. Those Jews, those Chinese, those West Indian tinnytintin-tack trash, and all those Communists want use black to shape their own culture. Man, I agree. I'm joining. I'm running down the road in Wolverhampton East with you, and Lewisham with you, and Hackney with you, and Manchester outer-ringway Hyde district, because civil rights 'I-had-a-dream' for the skinny weaklings, sir, because 'black-is-beautiful' just another rip-off Jew scheme, because 'keep-the-faith-brother' some red Trot swindle to make black into class weapon – white Marxists exploit colour – black body bullets for cracking the capitalist edifice.

. . . That's why I volunteer to join the National Front, sir, man.

. . . I'm not trying insult your . . .

. . . I told you I've never been in no monkey house in my life.

. . . No sir, no syphilis is in my head.

. . . Don't drink heart-attack whisky. And palm wine don't grow off trees in Southall.

... I am telling the word's truth.

... I do not lie.

[*He retreats away from the desk.*]

... I'm doing it with all the dignity I got left. I'm no special case. I'm voicing with the voice of thousands, sir.

[*He lifts up his arms to protect himself. He tumbles away to the wall.*]

... I'm your side, man, sir. Singing the same song. You got Jews ain't yer? You got Cypriots ain't yeh? You got Irish? You got Lebanese?

[*He holds his forearm tightly against his neck. He is being squashed back, half-throttled aganist the wall.*]

... OK! ... OK! ... OK!

[*He eases away from the wall. The pressure is off. He chokes back his breath. He smartens himself up. Wipes the sweat away. Reaches for the glass-glaze door.*]

... Fine, sir ... you keep that £3 money I sent in good faith sir. What? True word I'm saying. What I get? Don't hit me, man. True word I got to give you it was. Dis-de-dat-dem-dum nigger wog? Who me, sir? Frankly sir, man, you let me down!

[*A book wings at his head. He ducks and eases out through the glass-glaze door.*

Later. GABRIEL *takes off his jacket as he comes out of the blockaded barrier door. He sits on the pavement outside the door.*

He sits.

A light switches off in front of the glazed door inside.

Footsteps.

And the barricaded door opens. And closes again. And the snap of a strong lock in place. The footsteps pause.

The light is different. GABRIEL *glances up.*]

GABRIEL: ... I'm not parked on your property now am I now? I'm just lounging like they say now. It's only me, sir, man.

[*The steps walk away.* GABRIEL *is different. The confident Lagos charm has faded. White urban shadows rule.*]

... Find you find yourself little bit scared, sir? I was saying true word. I was saying I'm on your side. See the same light and all. What scared you, mister? Little Port Harcourt lad palm wine gone runny in his head?

[*The footsteps stop. Pause. Hear the steps turn.*]

... All right you feared of nothing. O K. Smash my face in? Aw you tried done that haven't you man?

... Want? Yearh well, maybe I haven been sitting out here coming to thinking about the world's money. Remember how I told you of the 800 million pounds running loose in Britain every week? Perhaps it is not much of a consolation to me but I have a way of concluding maybe that £799 million, 999 thousand and 997 belong to somebody else. But I sure could do with that last £3 of mine which I sent to you.

... Go fuck my ass, man, sir? I didn't quite catch the last – I see. Yearh ...

... Well, I was considering putting that £3 to good use. Try to make my way to the International Stores shop. Go through the old routine. Six-pack of canned beer, darling, thank you. She thinks I'm just another West Indian rum and coke head and she fetches out the cans of Red Stripe. I say no sir, lady, I mean a six-pack of Newcastle Brown and a bottle of cheap German sweet white wine for the yellow splits.

... Maybe true word, I was pulling you a little of the cotton wool inside. I thought you'd prefer hear the shine on top of the shoes, and not study the socks peering out my heel and toes. Were you impressed by the nigger done well?

... That's right, sir. Like thunderclouds raining down the sky full of dog shit you were impressed! Huh?

[*The footsteps walk on.*]

... Don't be in such a hurry there. It's all right. I'm leaving. Like I was always leaving someplace and getting to another place and little voice breathes in your ears – 'Wrong place park your ass, buddy buddy'. First fact I know my father brings me into this country when I was not yet walking. And it don't take immigration less than four months to sort

our family out. And two of them four months we're in the
old immigrant dog-pound, Dalston, on the grounds that my
father got his passport to sleep on a private citizen's bed, but
my mother never has, and as for me – I'm an injurious em-
barrassment. The sisters got photos on my father's passport.
OK by them. But first they have to inform my father he
ain't so much as married to my mother according to their
records. Then they turn to me and say, 'We have no absolute
evidence according to the child ownership statutes, that, one,
you are the child of this couple and, two, that you rightly
and properly and lawfully do exist.' Not quite having learned
the ropes enough to stand, altho I could crawl, I gave them
a bit of my black voodoo Ogwe divination lip.

... Yearh, it don't commence easy do it? There was my
mother in one detention centre. There was the sisters in
another. My father having the true word passport and done
all his forms right doing the work – catching wild cats on
Dalston bomb sites for the Council. Sixpence a cat and
threepenny piece a rat. It took us all three years before
they'd allow us together under one roof.

... Since I was at school I can understand the black dreams,
church and Christians and getting it right, and asking all the
time why this white man is the son of God, and that white
woman seen fit to mother him from his cradle. Come the day
I said to my schoolteacher, 'Well, teach, far as I can find it,
it is all white and no black or yellow nowhere, how come it
this way?' She said to me, 'First there was Noah, and he had
had his ark all fitted up nice and dry. Had himself two sons,
forget their names, and they're both sit there beside him in
the long grass one day. And Noah fall asleep. Wind blow a
dance. And one son sees Noah's skirts blown up over his
waist, and his private parts come up to see them naked. The
first son laugh and think it a great joke. The second son don't
at all. He put the old man's skirt in order in the respectable
manner it was. When the old man woke, he heard what the
first son did. And he banished him for ever. And the boy
turned the colour of brown sugar. And forever more,' said

the teacher, 'all you black kids result of that division.' 'I see,'
said I. But I didn't in truth. I lay up in bed that night and
watched out at the starlight. And asked myself – we all black
kids now just because one whitey fart in history book looked
up his old father's legs and laughed!?

... You don't want to believe all that talk I had about Ogwe
and Ibaa village life and hairy trees which havoc vengeance
on you do a deed wrong on someone. I forget those names of
the spirits in the forest. My father said they were there,
when he was dying in the hospital, he said the harpy birds
and the water-spirit women were at the bottom of his bed.
When the doctor come along in the evening and shake his
head and glance at the charge sheet at the bottom of the bed,
sometimes, too, I like to think my old man was watching
water sprites and the hairy trees. Before the hairy charge
sheet ripped him away, he said to me, 'Go out and get your
job, save it, and you back Gabriel, you got your home in
West Africa.' I wanted to say, 'Sure Dad, I'll do that.' But
instead I said, 'There ain't no home in that dream.' And
there ain't much of a home in this dream here. You see, he'd
been unemployed last ten years of his life. Weren't ever any
chance of a pension anyway for him. And he fought in the
British Nigerian Infantry. Just like those hairy trees and *nsi*
the water sprite and Noah's bad son done the laughing.

... And I thought you'd understand, you think as I do find
it, I told you I was with a white woman, my white wife
Janine, all these recent times. I'm ashamed. You did understand that didn't you, sir?

... Quite right. I say so, too. It was shaming. Shames her.
Shames it on me. Right?

... In the first instance she didn't get pregnant. First she
lives with me here in Southall. I say goodbye to the sisters.
First these men from the Commission of Racial Equality
dropping in and say, 'Be a good thing you both settle down.
Put you on the Southall Council list. Then you can get
pregnant and claim high priority. And the Commission
makes representation to the council. And the council become

embarrassed. And the board hint darkly about labour domi-
nated council prejudice. And in no time Gabriel you can
hump the whole queue.' And Commission of Racial Equality
notched up great victory. If I'd had a strong hand like you
sir hear that sort of stuff. Say to them, 'Cut all that white
liberal crap bending over backwards destroying two cultures
at one.' I should have had my head examined for being so
dumb. I should have gone to jail overnight for shacking up
with Janine.

. . . Mind, it was Janine one wanted to clinch it all in church
with me. And I was one who wanted to cool it, lying around
all day make-believing I was talking easy and loose, you
know, like dem West Indian lazynothins, sayin to ma woman,
'De cost of livin gettin oh so high, de cost of lovin make me
want to cry.'

. . . First I didn't use my noddle. Then soon light come.
What future Janine got in my black world? And she was
saying to me, 'Go on out now, do your nining to fiving hard
day's driving and bring me back my money on Friday night,
Gabriel. Go to flicks, Gabriel. Sunday bingo got a Hotpoint
Automatic raffle, Gabriel. Work like a black, Gabriel. I'll
feed you white bread, Gabriel.'

. . . It was no skin off me to find out where the jobs going
was. Down the bottom of the pack, down the fetchit and
digit, down the scrape it and washit. At least you know where
you are. And I was tired of the indignity because I was I
thought 'some day'. And I'd been looking for ten months
with no success. Ring, ring. 'About that job, sir?' 'Come
round rightaway, son.' Knock, knock. I'm shiny black smiling
me, sir. 'Sorry, boy, that job taken long time gone.'

. . . And this Kingston friend Abdul Jerry call by me when
Janine out. 'How yo liffin, mon shit? Dis white wooman on
teh strits fer yeh? Yer pimpin she, mon?' And I was in mind
to invite him to kick-in-the-crutch festival when he said –
'Yer wan be rich yer let-go shit yer?' He had an ear for a
good job on the Southall Disposal Squad – they like to call
themselves that – in truth they just ordinary dustbin team

they been all their lives. Abdul say – 'Fockit, mon, et'll cost yer kindating.' 'How much, Abdul?' Abdul – 'Hunnerd crinkles up fron, mon, fer teh priffelej, mon'. And so I started on mornings. 'Black bastard like you, Gabriel, (they liked to call me "black bastard") black bastard like you, once you're in wiv us boy, you're in.' Time pass, and I notice the others used to huddle when they totted up the lead-weight once a month. Then it was another huddle when they did the cast-iron weight. 'Don't worry your little black snot, tell you what, we'll give you the chrome-plate concession and 2 per cent of the fine-quality brown cardboard tally. How's that, Gabriel?'

... I thought I had my rights and I went to the General Workers' Union representative and I said I was being robbed. He turned round to me and asked me was it true I paid £100 for the job. In that case I obtained the job by bribery, and the local standing committee would recommend I leave the union forthwith. 'You're a rank and file troublemaker you are, Gabriel. This is no genuine grievance against your brother worker. It's mutiny.'

... I never did give Janine her £100 back. I didn't see much future in the fine-quality brown cardboard concession, and my mates put me in Coventry. Of course, they made a joke about, and said it wasn't Coventry really, it was 'Wolverhampton East you're in Cocoa', and I never went back on the cart.

... I had noticed only too much Abdul Jerry lingering around the flat. Then he comes up one day says there's a decent black-collar job on the docks down at Rotherhithe. I don't want no black-collar job. 'Yes you do man, dockers' union man, free cross-channel tickets, occasional crate of rum fall on your big toe, man.' One thing about Abdul – his imagination. I got the posting. Then the convenor man from the Dockers' Union call me in. He says, 'You only got the job because you scraped inside the TUC black quota.' 'So?' I says. 'So you're here on sufferance.' 'How come, sir?' 'Because when the next wage hike goes in, that quota will be

halved,' he said. 'That's not sufferance, that's sufferation,'
I told him. It took six months for the wage hike to come in.
Forty-two of us got the axe. Not a whitey among us. Before
I left I walked up to that convenor. I said, 'Fuck you white
ashhole commie!' He shrugged. He said, 'Fair enough,
brother'.

[*The footsteps are walking away.*]

... That is why – what brought me – to come to you, sir.
Why I sent in my application, sir.

[*The footsteps continue and fade away.*]

... Maybe if I'd made it all sound funnier for you. Like it in
a sing-song voice with a reggae shuffle? Cricket boot white
rings round my eyes and mouth? Yearh?

... I could tell you about Ralphie. Make you laugh. He's my
son. Janine and mine. Like to catch a good belly-laugh, sir?

[GABRIEL *rattles it along with a coon tone.*]

... You recall I said about Abdul Jerry, Jerry around my
pitch. I come home and I find him in bed with Janine. And
there's Ralphie in the cot. I said, 'Put your pants on black-
beard, is shit coming up fast!' And Abdul moving like a
horse-fly. Here there. Duck there. 'Try this.' Window break.
Elmore James record collection falling out the drink tray.
'Hoo ha! Never knew you had false teeth, Abdul!'

[GABRIEL *shadow boxing. Tippytoe Tomsteps.*]

... In come the blue honks. Out come the handcuffs. 'You
the tart belong to these types?' Janine scream. Abdul's pants
falling down. I'm in the van and kicking. Abdul on top of me
and kicking. Janine in other car. Horns gunning. '*Where's
Ralphie?!*'

[GABRIEL *slows down. Tic-tac dragster fade away.*]

... And we driven off, and somebody kicked the front door
shut with Ralphie locked inside screaming on his back alone.

... I don't know how long Ralphie cried. Me and Abdul was
booked in for the night. Nobody allow us talk about the kid
locked up all night no one with him. Magistrate was called for
nine o'clock call. Janine, she collapsed in her cell. No matter
what she did or said, she screaming about Ralphie alone, they

said, 'Yes dear, in good time dear, those two blacks your pimps, are they dear?'

. . . It was six o'clock in the morning. And this Social Worker come in the cell. She don't exactly come in. Stand in the door. And said, 'Your Ralphie is fine. A neighbour broke down the door. He's in Shelter's Kiddie Emergency Night Centre. If I were you, Mr Nkoke, you could issue a summons against the authorities for wilful neglect under the Child Care Act.'

. . . After we got fined, we had ten days to get the money. I go up to blue meany number one outside the court – I say, 'That kid could have been left to die!' He say, 'He'd be better off dead than with you!'

. . . Abdul pull me away from the policeman. Took me aside and said, 'You in too much beef, Gabriel, yeh en swayin, Gabriel. All white babylon is a war a go hot, mon. Too much sufferation got into yer, yer focking blown it an yerve got whitey shit up to yer throat OK? OK? Gabriel? Look mon, I'll heff Ralphie, I'll tekk on Janine too, mon, yer in a knot see, go away and do what yer heff to do, go on back home Nigerian nigger kindating, go on, mon. Tink of Garvey, mon? Garvey dyin bread focking broke, mon, in West Kensington. Go on back home becos yer got one, before all war a go hot in dis country.'

. . . Yearh I thought. And who put Garvey in prison? Reggae black freaks. Black zionists percenting soulsound. And ELVIS SUCKS BLACK ROCK. Yearh.

. . . An I try the Nigerian Consulate, man. I'm sayin, 'Here's up country me goin down black Africa roots fast, you know.' [*He breaks into pidgin.*] 'En got equality palaver here, sir, got to *sabe* white books, got no chance for to be *oge* for I'm own house, sir, an I'm comin home, sir, like a man go fit stay all time for him house, sir, sir. An I'm prepared to walk along the road, with meh cassava an meh yams an meh palm-wine bottley, an face he Death with the *ju-ju* spirit when he Death come for . . . An I still got the true word pidgin meh ole man gave me.' . . . 'Mister Nkoke? It is by no means certain we can offer you a Nigerian passport. As we understand it you are eligible for a UK passport. Have you applied under the 1973 Immigration Act for the grant of amnesty?' 'No, sir, not me. I'm a Nigerian.' 'Well, Mister Nkoke, if you leave this country there is no guarantee the authorities will allow you back in.' 'I en comin back. I'm on my way back black homelan.' 'I'm sorry, Mister Nkoke, even if we supply you with a temporary visa, there is no guarantee you will be allowed to stay in Nigeria.' I forget what he . . . my ears goin mad . . . him say – oh something bout – I'm the new type of man. I'm neither here. Nor neither there. I'm some kind of universal alien. I'm an *inalienable alien*, him say. I belong but I'm not wanted, him say. An I shouted an came on with meh Ogwe lip an meh pidgin patter, him say how sorry him is, oh yearh . . .

. . . Yearh . . . an it bites now don't it . . .

. . . Yeh dyin of yer own gods an yer gods ain lissenin . . .

. . . An me thinkin somewheres at the bottom of the pile there must be udders . . .

. . . And I was walking along the road with my hands in my pockets. My girl Janine now with jah bum Abdul. And Ralphie with his Nescafé nose. Something deciding in me.

. . . And I was walking along this road with my hands in my pockets. Nothing else in them. And I was walking by one of your meetings and when I stopped to listen, yearh, for a moment, it was 'You Dust My Broom', you know.

. . . It's about *take*.

. . . *Taking* Mumbles Horton music giving it to white voice. *Taking* fella like Abdul and feeding him dilute with Janine. And little Ralphie and his colour halfway there already to what you are. Yearh. And nothing left to *take* because you took it all, sir, man. Yearh. Nothing left but what you can't even give away – your *poverty*: I'll buy that. Nothing except what you can't even throw away – your *hatred* and your *fascism*: and I'll buy that. So . . .

[*Mock Nazi salute.*]

Zeig Heil bullshit! And I'll buy that one!

END

For the West (Uganda)

For the West (*Uganda*) was first presented at the Theatre Upstairs, London, on 18 May 1977; and at the Cottesloe stage, National Theatre, on 13 August 1977, with the following cast:

Field Marshal Doctor Idi Amin 'Dada', President for Life of Uganda	RUDOLPH WALKER
Major George 'Amos' Todd	BASIL HENSON
Greville William Allnutt	ROGER MILNER
Isaid Dem Ala-Messid Jalli	RENU SETNA
Voice of the President's Secretary	FUMI LAYO

Directed by Nicholas Wright
Designed by Anne-Marie Schöne

'Now I have had this dream . . . I know the day I am going to die, and who does this to me. Prophet John has told me, also. That is why it must be top secret I'm afraid . . .'

FIELD MARSHAL DOCTOR IDI AMIN 'DADA'
PRESIDENT FOR LIFE OF UGANDA
23 August 1973

CHARACTERS

FIELD MARSHAL DOCTOR AL-HAJJI IDI AMIN 'DADA', DSO, MC, VC, CBE, COMMANDER-IN-CHIEF OF THE ARMED FORCES, MINISTER OF DEFENCE, AND PRESIDENT FOR LIFE OF UGANDA

MAJOR GEORGE 'AMOS' TODD
GREVILLE WILLIAM ALLNUTT
ISAID DEM ALA-MESSID JALLI
VOICE OF THE PRESIDENT'S SECRETARY

The characters who appear in the dream sequence, and who belong to the President's imagination, are called ANGUS FRASER and SINDI BARU

ACT ONE	Idi's Dream
ACT TWO	Kampala Real
ACT THREE	Incidental Flashback

ACT ONE

It is IDI's *dream.*

    [IDI *is asleep in medalled splendour. A long balcony view. Nothing obstructs the view. It is beautiful. There are British cartoons framed against the walls. A large desk. An intercom. Various white plastic soft chairs.*

    Intercom on.]

VOICE [*indicate dream*]: Yes, Mr President.

IDI [*indicate dream*]: What you got out there?

VOICE: The British Delegation, Mr President. A Forward Delegation come prepare for next month talks on compensation.

IDI: What their names?

VOICE: Major George Amos Todd. Dr Angus Fraser. Mr Sindi Baru. You will find all the necessary papers on your desk.

IDI: You send them in right away.

VOICE: At once, Mr President.

    [*Fade for the dream sequence. Lights again.* AMOS *and* ANGUS *and* SINDI *carry* IDI *on stage. They carry him seated on a giant board. They lower* IDI.

    The MAJOR *is in uniform.* FRASER *in white shirt Commonwealth Office diplomacy bespoke.* IDI *effusive.*]

AMOS [*indicate dream*]: Sir!

IDI: My old Commander friend!

AMOS: That's right, sir!

IDI: The Major Amos who taught us all how to put the famous Sandhurst British boot in.

AMOS: King's African Rifles, sir, out in Karamoja. And how we smashed the Suk and the Askari, sir!

IDI: B Company No. 4 King's Africans. And that night I was sergeant we took those members the Central Legislative Assembly out fact-finding they call it, and in the night a lion creep in and eat all their underwear.

AMOS: I right recall how you polished him off, that lion, sir. From the top of the Land Rover –

IDI: Only damn safe place to be

AMOS: Fair good to best aim that was, sir.

IDI: Big ·375 rifle. Up the throaty. Those bullets could throw a man . . . Who we got here?

AMOS: Dr Angus Fraser from the Commonwealth Office. East Africa speciality. Eight years' service in Nairobi.

IDI: What rank you have in the British Commonwealth Office?

ANGUS [indicate dream]: Sir, Mr President . . . First Secretary (East African Advisory Board) and direct liaison with the Assistant Under-Secretary of State, Foreign and Commonwealth Office. The Under-Secretary and I are –

IDI: Very pleased to have you here. Hope you didn't have long to wait. Some peoples think it not safe to come here see Amin.

ANGUS: It is an honour to visit your beautiful country, Mr President. What Winston Churchill called 'the pearl of Africa'.

AMOS: And . . . Mr Sindi Baru. Delegate to the United Nations High Commission for Refugees. Representative of the Disenfranchised Asian Communities –

IDI: Dis –

SINDI [indicate dream]: Communities throughout the world, sir, not of Africa alone –

IDI: Is that so?

SINDI: It is an honour, Mr President, to be presented to you thus.

IDI: Good man, good man, what are you?

SINDI: Pakistani, sir.

IDI: I like all Pakistanis. Some are still here because they wanted Uganda passports of their own volition.

SINDI: I have never before been to your country.

IDI: You would at all times have found it most hospitable –

SINDI: I am a British passport-holding Sudanese resident, sir. I have lived twenty years in Khartoum.

[Dream indication ceases. Lights come up.]

IDI: Dr Fraser you in Nairobi all that time you say?

ANGUS: I was, sir. And my wife had the pleasure to work on the

96

Board of the Kikuyu Karinga Education Association during my term of commission.

IDI: What? ... That's right ... That's good ... Old friend Amos here remember. We King's African Rifles smashed into those tribal groups flirting with what the British called 'Mau Mau'. I don't want Jomo say to me you just white man's imperial black ass man. Jomo think differently from me. But we the same. I'm a brother. Not going to take any lip from American church leader.

ANGUS: Eh ... who, sir?

IDI: Jomo threw out white American missionary for speaking renegade Russian author. From the pulpit. I do same. I've never read this Solzhenitsyn's rubbish. You read his rubbish?

SINDI: No, sir.

IDI: Most likely western propaganda in desperate need of a stooge. Author runaway hate his own country love his million Swiss francs he got. And trick him up with Nobel prize award and say he's a martyr. Nothing special about award. Sartre famous French writer turned award down, rubbish. I have a VC ... here it is ... Queen didn't give it me. I'm not without pride. I made it. I give it myself big parade in a silver box. I'm not ashamed. Only the humiliated accept awards any kind. You read this Russian rubbish?

SINDI: No, sir. Definitely.

IDI: Taking no lip from any Christian teacher. You heard of that man Denis Hills Mr Denis Hills silly man: Two years ago of the hundred forty-six teachers National Teachers' College, Kampala, there were six black Ugandan teachers, the rest Asians I got nothing against them but, until I come by and see this how can you study from this what chance black Uganda got to learn! And ... Mr Denis Hills I liked Denis I showed him the law of this country and I advised him about 'Black Nero' whatever that may mean, and writing 'village tyrant' he write, and set him free, give him Mr Callaghan, famous British subject retrieved from black horror camp jail about to be shot in the front page of the *Daily Express*. All this way Callaghan personal to get Denis

I know Jim well, and in five minutes Hills Mr Hills publishing whole text of the book in a British Sunday paper, and I leave it to James Callaghan who was the Foreign Secretary to say what a dirty trick it is. I'm proven right.

AMOS: Mr President, sir – ?

IDI: I was busy talking.

AMOS: You were, sir.

IDI: Now I ceased.

AMOS: If I may bring to your attention, sir –

IDI: I am Big Daddy 'Dada' Idi Amin and I don't mind it at all. I am Chancellor of Makerere University. Holder of MC, VC, and CBE (Conqueror of the British Empire, that one). Israeli medal of bravery, holder of famous Israeli 'wings' honorary, DSO and full Brigadier-General of all my armies. Nothing serious about that. I laugh at medals. Laugh at fake colonial pomp and glory. Marx said every man should have a few medals keep him cheerful. Commander-in-Chief of my Simba Tigers Ladies' Suicide Battalion. Permanent Deep Diver Boss and water-wings consultant for the Ugandan Army Frogmen Division. Acting-host and chairman for the OAU summit in Kampala, Uganda, 1975. And you are here to see me, well, I give a big welcome!

AMOS: Thank you, sir, I am sure that –

IDI: Anything you want ask.

SINDI: May I put forward the th –

IDI: I hold no hands back.

ANGUS: There is a formal order of precedence with regard to the matters in hand, sir, namely –

IDI: I am a good friend of Britain. Great Britain.

ANGUS: The . . . eh . . . prime consideration, Mr President, for this meeting is to lay down ground rules and preliminary procedure for the Kampala Conference in the forthcoming month.

IDI: I shall have returned from my two meetings first I'll be at the UN Assembly in New York for a crucial vote upon Israel – motion of censure – then I shall be back in Dar-es-Salaam for final Angola Summit jointly make censure of Chinese, Russian and American imperialist interference in African affairs.

ANGUS: If I may, sir – our function here today is to set out all the itinerary for a joint Uganda/UK settlement on the problem of compensation for those exiled Asians *circa* 1972 and for those business and or registered companies who can rightfully show loss of earnings, fallen ratio of production and considerable economic hardship, particularly in the field of wage structures honoured, meanwhile the firm's production has virtually ceased, and in other fields such as inability to maintain stocks and equipment, the servicing of machinery etc., and the required coal and gas reserves I am thinking particularly of i.e. the mining areas in the south . . . and if I might say so – the normal preferential treatment Uganda has traditionally offered to British mining concessions.

[*Pause.*]

IDI: . . . Yes.

ANGUS: Therefore, sir, I am instructed by senior colleagues at the Defence Ministry taking full cognisance of your enthusiasm for a quick and just settlement to these outstanding matters –

IDI: Uganda always pays its debts.

ANGUS: – and continued relations thus. All forms, all claim forms that is, if I may suggest what has already been laid down in Whitehall, and passed on to your departmental Head of Asian Affairs; if you will recall – HMG has only maintained a token residence at Commission House, Kampala, somehow, in this confusion your departmental Chief did not inform Whitehall that these papers had arrived.

IDI: Sometimes not all things come down the pipe, but I clearly remember my appropriate Minister had already acquainted himself with this paper. I don't know the full reason why he never did reciprocate with your side, or with Commission House, he should have done, on his own volition, but instead, I think he handed in his formal resignation on board Sudanese Airlines 727 by way of radio contact with my airport staff.

ANGUS: I see, sir.

IDI: I tell you one thing, when any Minister of mine wants to act fast move quickly you know, by Christ, there is no stopping them.

ANGUS: And of course, reprinted we find this same Memorandum in the House of Commons sessional papers, eh – papers 196, sir.

IDI: But what do I mind, I bear no beef against any of them, they go abroad, send wife and kids up front first class take a little bit of Uganda currency to Switzerland, earn a fat fee from a capitalist paper saying what a monster I am, what can I do? I laugh a little. It makes me feel sad. All leaders are betrayed, it is the sour side of the top.

ANGUS: May I . . . ask here and now . . . sir . . . it is understood we keep an open-ended arrangement as to how and when the proposals forthcoming for compensation are to be paid i.e. there is no hard and fast rule for immediate payment whilst certain companies may need time to gear up their potential should these payments be made in a staggered form. I particularly refer to manufactured goods with production rundown by the natural course of events and where compensation over a long period i.e. directly related to national cash flow and Ugandan Government profit-sharing schemes –

IDI: I . . . am following you closely.

ANGUS: If I . . . putting it very plainly, sir . . . eh . . . if such profits come about with world market currency payments, the unit of distribution is one very much of mutual benefit to both countries, or say – the dollar market, euro or IMF or petro related OPEC currency is swimming in an up-stream direction, again it is monetary sense to seek joint benefits for both parties –

IDI: You want to ask me if I like sterling or dollars or marks I like it all I say.

ANGUS: I need hardly add the rider that – production of manufactured goods accelerates with new government participation from Ugandan Legislative Powers, and I am sure all such profits will have all the time in the world to select their monetary unit of exchange.

IDI: It's called finding the good pig and bringing it on back home, Dr Fraser.

ANGUS: Well, sir, shall we say we do agree, for openers, on open-ended discussions on friendly terms?

IDI: Of course! That is why we are here!

AMOS: Absolutely! Quite so!

IDI: Why isn't the High Commissioner here? I'd like him to hear that.

AMOS: Sir, I will convey that to the Commissioner this evening.

IDI: Why don't he come here now?

AMOS: I believe he has already expressed his regret. The confusion lay in the fact that he was, as I was, under the impression these preliminary talks would be in the company of your Ministers. Not with you personally –

IDI: My Ministers half the time down town looking up their Shell shares and changing dollars on the black market. I do all the work here.

AMOS: Quite so, sir.

IDI: I do everything I can. I bar them from the golf club until the weekends, I forbid them hiding in other embassies doing unscrupulous talks behind my back, I put the Turkish bath out of bounds until the evening, and if my police see them inside any one of those brothels – all brothels have been banned – their wives are told promptly. I want enlarged specification for each and every claim against the Ugandan Government.

ANGUS: That is laid down in the Government White Paper Memorandum, sir –

IDI: And I need a reciprocal amount of time for Legislative Council appointed business experts to analyse each specification –

ANGUS: Thank you sir ... no prima facie accountability, all claims subject to full inquiry, reciprocal time allotted, no forms sanctioned without this prior working agreement.

IDI: Now what was it was this 'open-ended discussion on friendly terms' Dr Fraser, you mentioned?

ANGUS: If I may put them in order of precedence –

IDI: That's right –

ANGUS: Item one, sir –

IDI: Item one . . . then . . .

ANGUS: One, channelling funds from UK through the offices of various societies.

IDI: All these things come under open-ended discussion on allied friendly terms?

ANGUS: I'm about to bring to your attention item number one, sir –

IDI: How many items you got written down there?

ANGUS: Channelling funds . . . sir . . . item one, sir . . . various societies both countries unilaterally agree to i.e. – World Council of Health, United Nations Appeal Fund, Church Foundations, Red Cross, Children's Funds and UNESCO.

IDI: I like UNESCO, singers, actors, all famous people running round headless trying improve the lot of those others who want. I liked Red Cross urgent health missions to India and relief famine and flood environmental good deeds and – you got the next item?

ANGUS: Item two – sir . . . eh . . . all concomitant matters relating to cessation . . . of British aid to Uganda –

IDI: I am big friend of UK I want all that aid back, and if I see it coming in the front door Idi pass them back big hallo and gladhand, and I understand Callaghan and the rest see sense; no use cutting off arm of best kith and kin UK got, whole of Africa, long after South Africa sunk under its own sewage, Uganda remain best friend of the Queen.

ANGUS: Further, according to the Memorandum – item three, it will be discussed under close and friendly terms a re-defining of the border interests *vis-à-vis* Sudan, Kenya, Zaire and Tanzania.

IDI: Fine by me, want come down and check the borders make sure Uganda friends all round fine by me I'm not ashamed nothing to hide no secret Marxist guerrilla groups attacking Cabenda Dam or training walk in South West Africa, Namibia – what you got there?

ANGUS: Item, sir, four. There will be an informal précis, jointly signed, between heads of signature, namely of course, sir, yourself and our Foreign Minister, a précis of Soviet and Chinese intentions in East Africa.

IDI: Want think whole place crawled up to ears with silent Russians, keep great British public satisfied somebody is still outposting for them in their old colonial world ... I don't mind. I'm willing to do that for Her Majesty. Why not? What harm done? Only harm I ever see, next British Government in charge turn over whole précis you call it to the CIA ... what the hell, they say don't they Amos?

AMOS: They do indeed, sir.

IDI: I sign for that one.

ANGUS: Thank you, sir.

IDI: Give me the next number.

ANGUS: Five sir it is item five. There will be an open-ended discussion round table approach on Israeli pre-occupation with Sudan. Findings jointly and strictly kept secret, sir.

IDI: I like Israel. Nice people. Only I hate Zionists. Zionists creeping all over Sudan looking for trouble. I ignore them. Israel cannot extend borders where it is common affront to humanity. America knows that. I talk with anyone about Zionists in Sudan. Nothing nobody fear.

ANGUS: Item ... eh ... the return of the American Diplomatic Corps to Kampala.

IDI: Very good very welcome there was a little misunderstanding, like them all, bring their wives meet my wives, children get their swimming pools back, dollars always needed, that what so many peoples think back home in England they been brainwashed by the media, I like British media I understand it, but the people don't. And all of a sudden here is Idi Amin with a funny suit on covered in decorations, himself standing in front of the great British laughing public and he is talking about the new ambassador to Ghana to some such place nine out of ten viewers never heard of they don't know anything about Africa except for the fact most of the inhabitants are black length of their general knowledge, and this Idi saying here is the news that America sending Shirley Temple

famous film star to Africa as ambassador . . . and Idi saying
this is an outrage because next thing happen before he turn
round he standing at Entebbe airport with his medals with
the red diplomatic carpet rolled out for US President's new
representative in Uganda, and out step off the plane a six-
year-old midget in ringlets tapdancing and shaking her curls
and shouting about the animal knackers in her soup. And I'm
sitting up in my cabinet office with a conductor's stick and all
my cabinet of Ministers in the background humming 'The
Good Ship Lollipop' instead of 'Stars and Stripes Forever'
. . . don't make any mistake . . . I know Shirley Temple is
more than six years old now. I like being laughed at. Nice big
clean fun. No harm being done me. Lot of harm and ignor-
ance being done famous British audience in their shirt-sleeves
rolled up.

ANGUS: Item seven sir . . . the encouragement of tourism in
Uganda.

IDI: Welcome it . . . open hands . . . gladly . . . this is the most
beautiful place whole East Africa . . . show them round the
old native villages . . . the old Kabaka Palace . . . the water-
falls. Hunting fishing shooting, wild life, find herbs of all type
crocodiles on river trips voyages into the dark forest. And
play cards candle-light Ugandan music all the staff in white
jackets serving drinks and free mosquito nets those with
sensitive skins.

ANGUS: Eight, sir? . . .

IDI: Go ahead, man.

ANGUS: Round-table discussion on a formal visit to the UK,
for a second time, at the invitation of Her Majesty's Government.

IDI: Yes, sir.

ANGUS: To be agreed mutually the date and the usual protocol
with which, of course, sir, you are familiar.

IDI: With which.

ANGUS: And that, with your permission, Mr President, is the
outline of the future open-ended items the next month joint-
country meeting here in Kampala.

IDI: Only invitation for a visit to your country which I so love
I will accept is one from Her Majesty the Queen herself with
whom I already have had the honour of, and I might add, it
was she and she alone who recognized my authority here in
ten days after the fall of Obote. I am grateful to her for that.

ANGUS: I'm sure you are, sir.

IDI: Oh no I ain't that stupid, you just watch that ass licking,
trouble with you Englishers –

ANGUS: I am a Scot, sir – with respect –

IDI: You too damn pleasant. No use sitting around in this
world oh how you do nice to meet did you hear the weather
report is it cricket and whole damn place from Hong Kong to
Panama Canal kicking themselves with laughter. World
falling apart and Britain Great British Britain still saying
thank you when they boot you down the stairs of the club you
once used to own. Now you said to me just a minute you said
your superiors from the Defence Ministry same breath you
said your superiors are Commonwealth Office what are you
Dr Fraser?

ANGUS: I answer to your question, Mr President –

IDI: You CIA –?

ANGUS: No, sir.

IDI: I remember. My ears tell me. Nobody got two bosses
Whitehall one the Defence the other Commonwealth Office –

ANGUS: Naturally sir – in inter-departmental exchange I confer
with the Defence Minister. I remain a Commonwealth man,
nevertheless. With respect, if I may.

AMOS: Doesn't strike you, sir, as an MI6 man, does he, sir?
What?

IDI: I'm not jumping to conclusions, I have an open mind.

ANGUS: What I mean by senior colleagues, I meant – of course,
Military Whitehall is always eager to know what we're doing
in the Commonwealth office.

IDI: But I believe you I trust you . . . what was it you said you
are?

ANGUS: Liaison Officer for the Assistant Secretary of State, sir:
East Africa speciality.

IDI: Very high-up secretary. You are a British permanent secretary?

ANGUS: As permanent as I can make myself, sir.

IDI: I trust you. You are a good man. But . . . I want to know all the details . . . don't want an idiot minister from Kampala come along get it all wrong dates and all and I'm suddenly flying to a big United Nations plenipotentiary talks in New York you ever played American football?

SINDI: Eh . . . no sir.

IDI: Who do we have at the conference here for compensation next month?

AMOS: I think I can best answer that if I may, old chum –

IDI: Very well, *major* –

AMOS: Sir. I beg your pardon . . . eh . . . to begin with The Commonwealth Office, aside from the Minister, will have two economic advisers, the High Commissioner here and the Assistant Under-Secretary of State, Dr Fraser's senior, and at least one separate man for each of the broad and friendly based items on the White Paper Memorandum which Dr Fraser has already outlined. This will make a separate joint committee if you will, to be countered on your side, sir, with respect, with your own group of experts –

IDI: How many men?

AMOS: Well . . . I'd say HMG will have to provide a per head count before arrival *pro rata* the necessaries. No extra fat on the diplomatic bag. What were you thinking of, Mr President, in view of – ?

IDI: Nothing . . . nothing at all . . . really.

AMOS: I'll telephone London tonight sir, or even catch the overnight bag Dar-es-Salaam flight –

IDI: Not important at all – I like the Nile Hotel to have the correct number of rooms available.

AMOS: Qu . . . quite.

IDI: Popular hotel the Nile.

AMOS: Sir?

IDI: Most my Ministers tucking away six-course breakfast eight o'clock mornings until I banned them from here too.

AMOS: Absolutely.

IDI: Bedsheets . . . hot water . . . air-conditioning . . . piped TV . . . colour . . .

AMOS: I will see to it HMG provide per head count details.

IDI: How many Asians coming along next month?

SINDI: With your permission Mr President –

IDI: Yes yes what the use of talking like this when you are come here to collect money from me and I am ready to meet you and my bank is open with all its wealth you still talk about permission. I am a friend of the world.

SINDI: There . . . there will be four of us with a complement of secretarial staff. Two men from the United Nations Board of Inquiry into the plight of Asians based in Geneva, myself and a Swahili-speaking international lawyer from London.

IDI: Is he Asian?

SINDI: Although Pakistani by birth, he carries a British Indian dual nationality –

IDI: He ever been here?

SINDI: He has never set foot on Ugandan soil.

IDI: He is Indian?

SINDI: With respect he is British, in his capacity as spokesman for Asian compensation, sir.

IDI: I got more letters from Delhi drawerful stack high from Mr J. S. Mehta, additional Secretary of the Indian Ministry of External Affairs, he say there are 1,500 newly impoverished Indians I've thrown out, I write back and says yes quite true how much? He write back he don't believe I'm ready to pay. I write back say the cheque book in my hand. He write back say no money in Bank of Uganda. CIA inform him bunch of lies, it never stop with these Indians never do. And British newspapers tell lies to their bourgeois readers that every night I sit at home and study my Who's Who of black Africa titled *Who Dat*? I got news for the great British public, Africa full of a thousand million black souls still bleeding from those colonial wounds. You like the view from my window? No barbed wire on my window. You don't see any Mahdi gunmen with automatic rifles body-guarding me here this is a peaceful place. You seen my cartoons? . . . Seen – Trogg, Cummings (Cummings mad vindictive fascist dog I like him he is honest I have him in my house for a cup of tea), *Private Eye* famous monthly weekly of the British Isles obscene witticisms. Garland (who he?) don't know him, Emmwood, Heath (another relation I suppose), Scarfe, Marc . . . all the top cartoonists . . . all drawn me . . . What do you think Amos?

AMOS: Quite disgraceful British propaganda.

IDI: Smother the English with big bad Idi, smother the English with violent revolution in Portugal (five killed in one year that what they call violent BBC propaganda) smother everyone with what they call World Service smother the public with revolution all over the world in every country except the place where it matters, where it should be shown, in Belfast, seaside capital of Irish Republic don't belong to Britain anyway, each week nobody say ten men women and children die ten of them and the bombings and the murders oh no got to hide it all away behind big Dada Amin laughter, no one mention fact that America retain nuclear submarine bases in Ireland official secret word from Washington to London don't get out of Ireland, secret Kissinger Zionist talk about Ireland becoming the Cuba of off-shore Europe second Cuba for the Russians and hundreds of plain clothes SAS army thugs first they shoot a Catholic then they go down the road and shoot a Protestant then a war starts in the road and the army turns round to Whitehall says there you are what did we say we need more men here to keep conflict under control . . . Poor Big Daddy what he done to deserve all this. Everybody get bad publicity some of the time. I get it all the time. Then I said something nice about Hitler. Adolf Hitler German Führer of the united German peoples before the war ended in 1945, European war that is. I said something nice about him (there may not be so many nice things you can say about him) all of a sudden what I see I am saying in the papers – 'Hitler was right to burn six million Jews.' Who was right? I said that? I ask you, you look at those cartoons you read that sort of nonsense silly bugger say so what we in the King's African

Rifles used to call 'tommyrot'. Would the President of the OAU run around shouting about burning six million any peoples? Everything I've done! You have to understand my sense of humour, smile a bit, kid along the white man a bit, I have twenty children of my own ... five wives ... one just dead ... one new one just recent ... would you marry your daughter to a man like that who just burnt six million of them?

AMOS: Splendid stuff!

ANGUS: I wonder if I may ... return to my series of programme points for the coming top-level meeting here, Mr President?

IDI: That is right.

ANGUS: If I check them down, detail by detail, can I take that as your assurance?

IDI: You can.

ANGUS [*files out on knee*]: This list ... of companies is complete and, though there might indeed be deletions or voluntary withdrawals of claim, there will assuredly be no further additions.

IDI: I understand.

ANGUS: These are claims for UK firms seeking lawful compensation in excess of £100 million.

IDI: Uganda pays.

ANGUS: Sir?

IDI: Bank of Uganda pays.

ANGUS: I –

IDI: All debts to be honoured world wide. This is an honest country.

ANGUS: Of course, sir, naturally –

IDI: I pick up this phone here – and at the other end of the line is my Manager of the Bank of Uganda –

AMOS: Eh – *President*, sir.

IDI: My Manager – nobody is encouraged much in this country to raise themselves to the level of President or Brigadier, unless I approve the say-so. I ring him up I say go down the basement and open up the bomb-proof Swiss-installed gates Idi your President coming in for the big handout and he goes running down those stairs like I was a pedigree cross between

Al Capone and Jack the Ripper reason you get no specialist murderers like Jack the Ripper in Africa creeping about in the misty London streets knocking off prostitutes and cutting out their vaginas reason being there is no pressures here like the olden days in Great Britain you heard of Jack the Ripper Mr Sindi?

SINDI: Yes, sir.

ANGUS: May I commence, with respect, with the firm of Smith Mackenzie Ltd; a claim for £406,000 against Uganda for loss of trade due to the sudden dismissal of ninety per cent of their staff during the Economic Year of Uganda – ?

IDI: Uganda pay.

ANGUS: Mackinon and Bros, £229,000.

IDI: We pay.

ANGUS: Wigglesworth Co. Ltd, £778,000.

IDI: Any sum over half a million sterling claimed against Uganda, while I accept most probably, this claim here, waiting on the most intense and vigorous Ugandan investigation by my experts into this claim, any sum over half . . . paid out of the fifty-one per cent Ugandan Government stake, the relative profits from such will pay over a period of twenty years.

ANGUS: Ralli Bros, £800,000.

IDI: Don't know them.

SINDI: Asian cloth merchants, sir, and factories for cotton yarn processing, and plastic fibre marrying processes.

IDI: I am not unjust. Asian or otherwise. Why should I attack Asians. They will get their money.

ANGUS: Mitchell Cotts Co. Ltd, claim of £490,000.

IDI: Fine.

ANGUS: Jos. Hansen Ltd, £169,000.

IDI: Bank pays.

ANGUS: African Mercantile and East Coast Marine Corps, £224,000.

IDI: Yes. Bank pays in Ugandan currency except where I stipulate as otherwise. For all claims.

ANGUS: Twentsche Overseas Trading Corps, £355,000.

IDI: Yes. All German and allied Asian businesses get their money.

ANGUS: Brooke Bond, £900,000. Destroyed stock on 1971 books.

IDI: Famous British tea bags with little holes. Amos?

AMOS: Quite, absolutely.

ANGUS: Barclays Overseas (East African Division), a sum of £6,480,000.

IDI: That is quite separate. All that is frozen assets. All will be released in the appropriate currencies they are held in, or exchange units with a guarantee from Bank of Uganda. I am not a fool, I would like Barclays men come here and justify how many millions they saved by putting all this six million down in their London city accountings as losses against taxation – cut that item from your list, please, Doctor.

ANGUS: Certainly certainly. Now . . .

IDI: Then this all-important meeting come to a close.

[IDI *strides purposefully towards the door.* FRASER *makes an effort to pluck up courage as they all abruptly stand for* IDI.]

ANGUS: . . . Sir! . . .

IDI: We all finished now.

ANGUS: If I may, sir –

IDI: All talking done.

ANGUS: I –

AMOS: If sir, you could see your way to just one or two final points which, though of course being minor, the Under-Secretary when he arrives next month will have prepared notes on . . . Sir . . . ?

IDI: What more notes he got?

[ANGUS *and* AMOS *exchange looks.* AMOS *gently takes* IDI's *arm and strolls with him across to the desk.*]

AMOS: May I as an old friend . . . Field Marshal, sir . . . the whole question of aid is in Uganda's national interest –

IDI: Uganda don't need aid. Uganda got the help of all African black nations got Libya and USSR and Saudi Arabia and Palestine Liberation –

AMOS: I think Dr Fraser has a further point on this – if you will –

ANGUS: Sir, HMG has since the expulsion of Ugandan Asians reduced original aid in the region of annual three million pounds sterling to something barely accommodating wages for British National teachers through the Ministry of Overseas Development, and yet there is still a basic imbalance between the bi-national trade – standing at, in the order of, some twenty millions pound sterling value into UK against seven millions imported into Uganda –

IDI: Nobody give anything away three-quarters of that larger sum belongs to private trading profit between British-owned companies, what Uganda see out of that precious little but a pittance tax –

ANGUS: I'd also like to remind the Field Marshal that some nine million francs annually form an EEC Central Loan Subsidy to East Africa which UK makes an additional eighteen per cent commitment fee towards.

IDI: We done now?

ANGUS: I only wish to explore these basic facts, sir.

IDI: They explored now.

ANGUS: And you accept, generally speaking, these facts are correct, sir?

IDI: Correct, correct. I go now.

ANGUS: . . . Sir! . . .

IDI: What you have now?

ANGUS: One positive final item will be on the Under-Secretary's agenda –

IDI: It the final one.

ANGUS: Being, an attempt should be made to outline a bilateral agreement on the general safety of UK nationals in Uganda, there are . . . it stands at the most recent count some three hundred eighty-six UK passport immigrant cardholders. A number of missionaries working north at Mbale, and at Masaka, and at Lake Edward, and certain medical people, who receive their salaries through the Catholic Fund for Overseas Development.

[*He slumps in the chair behind the desk. The impatience has given way to a cumbrous drowsiness.*]

IDI: You come to see me. And I am here. Now you have finished all this and we set about the business with my Cabinet. First I talk to them. Then they talk to you. Then all the Under-Secretaries of State meet next month I could be called away in an instant on my travels. What are we saying what we doing here? For we should make a joint statement announce initial intentions to lay down procedure for big meeting –

ANGUS: With respect, this is precisely –

IDI: And tell the world whole world waiting for genuine positive action in the face of many crises what we say?

SINDI: If I may point out – I am not sure Dr Fraser being an Englishman can see it so clearly – this is an attempt to detail exactly the British commitment to Uganda, and to account for every aspect of British interests in order that both countries exactly reciprocate true understanding.

IDI: You write it down . . . An intelligent man . . . Intelligent Indian. I like Indians. This top-drawer level meeting terminated.

AMOS: Sir!

IDI: You all need long cold shower in the hotel. Is the tap running?

AMOS: Sir!

IDI: Tomorrow big treat I'll take you up the Nile show the crocs no show the crocs you you will not be afraid because I'll be with you I'll show all my military planning campaign to utterly destroy centre of Tel Aviv in one counter-stroke.

ANGUS: It would be a fascinating experience, Mr President.

IDI: Must understand I like Jews I wear this Star of David top Israeli medal I respect them the greatest fighters on earth. Goodbye.

[IDI *cordially shakes* ANGUS *and* AMOS *by the hand. And* SINDI. *As* SINDI *is the last to leave.*]

IDI [*indicate dream*]: No you . . . you can come back.

SINDI [*indicate dream*]: Me, sir?

IDI: I want to show I have the most cordial willing to spend more time than with any other particularly those Britishers

civil service gobblegook I like Britishers but it is the Indians
I must show my new face to. The kind face. I have no com-
plaint. I let all things pass. Then I hear that the British
Government complaining ten million pound a week sterling
smuggled out of the country to Jamaica and West Indies and
Kingston and India all sent back home and I am laughing.
Where did you think all the Uganda currency went up to
1972? It went out through the Post Office go down there any
Saturday morning you like I take you I could have shown you
what is in those fat envelopes? All this money going out to
India and Pakistan and the whole cash-flow currency of
Uganda bleeding a death.

SINDI: If I may point out, sir that –

IDI: I heard all that before. But I have forgiven. You are forgiven. You are a friend. Come in peace here. I'll show you
my children beside the swimming pool. All Indians clever
and resourceful. You heard of Prophet John? The great
prophet of my country? He come from Lugazi. My mother
loved a Muslim greatly from there. And I was born in Koboko
West Nile Province. My father was Kakwe. My mother was
a Lugbara. She ran away from him with me. She went from
one barracks to another, always with me, from Jinja to Buikwe
to Lugazi. I could speak Luganda and Kiswahili and Aruan
Sudanic. And I was the heavyweight champion of the British
army. Prophet John come to me, he say he can read into the
future. He can see into the other parts of the future where no
one else can penetrate. I ask him Prophet what going to pass?
With me? He say you are going to die, and a hero and a national Africa all African hero you'll become. So, I pick you out
from the others because it is necessary to show this hand of
friendship broad big as Africa even to an Indian. I don't hate
them I think they work hard but they must work for the
country in which they thrive and not against it. You wouldn't
like all Bagandese take over rice production in India and send
it all back to Masaka? My dream is, say the Prophet, Idi's
dream – I will know the hour of my end and the exact minute
and who done it. You like Agatha Christie novels?

SINDI: *Mr President, I have a message for you from a number of old friends of yours outside of Uganda* – Muhammed Hussein, and Colonels M. Arach, A. Langoya, Akwango, Ojok, Abwala, Ayumi, Ekirring, P. Obol, O. Ogwal; the soldiers and friends of Lugbara, the men and women of Mbarra, former Prime Minister of Uganda, Kiwanua; Vice-Chancellor of Makerere University, Kalimuzo; Governor of the Bank of Uganda, Mubiru; the Chief-Justice of Uganda, Benedicto Kiwanuka and Archbishop Luwum.

IDI: All these men are missing or dead.

SINDI: It is their message to you, sir –

> [SINDI *holds a small pistol in his hands. He stands close up to* IDI *and grips the butt with both hands for firmness. He holds it steadily and as far away from his eyes as he can.* SINDI *pulls the trigger. No percussion.*
>
> *Blackout. Sound of loud breathing. Lights up.*
>
> IDI *is in his cot bed. The dreamer is sleeping.*]

ACT TWO

Jinja bungalow.

> [*It is an untidy front room. Ceiling fan rotates. Stick furnishings. Cabinet files. Impression of litter and haste.*
>
> MAJOR GEORGE 'AMOS' TODD *enters in full uniform. He sits behind a desk and lays out his papers from a portfolio. He takes off his hat and rings a stand-bell before him.*
>
> *Shouting and shoving from outside. A manacled 'ANGUS FRASER' wearing filthy light clothes with a couple of days' stubble is shoved into the room. The door slams behind him. The time is as close to the present as we can assume.*]

AMOS: ... Ah, there you are. Good morning.

ANGUS: Good?

AMOS: Here we are, at last.

ANGUS: Where ... are we?

AMOS: First of all shall we take things easily ... first steps et cetera ... explore the terrain if you will ...

ANGUS: Who in hell are you?

AMOS: To begin with, I'm British ... eh ... set your mind at rest.

ANGUS: I want to use a telephone right away –

AMOS: Aah ...

> [*He holds up the mouthpiece of the machine* 'ANGUS' *grabs at on the desk. No sound.*]

... Dead as a door-nail, what? Only phone you ever find working here belongs to the Wabenzi; no sound at all, what?

ANGUS: I demand ...

AMOS: Let's sit down shall we? Little more civilized. I'm sorry about the ... eh ... cuff-links. I did request – but trouble with finding the key – and Towilli is not here, he is up country chasing through bush looking for an idiot Asian accidentally come over the Kenya border and says he lost his way, poor sod, where were we?

ANGUS: I demand help. Who are you from?

AMOS: I think you'll find . . . I'm the one responsible for most of the questioning here.

ANGUS: Why am I here?

AMOS: Start at starters shall we –

ANGUS: Are you in a position to help me?

AMOS: According to all this tommyrot written down – worst typing since Caterham School Corps tents and provisions inventory.

ANGUS: Who is Towilli?

AMOS [*more to himself and the papers*]: I'm ready, are you?

ANGUS: And most important of all – where am I?

AMOS: I am George 'Amos' Todd. Major. Uganda has been my stamping-ground for many years. And I have the benefit of direct communication with the Ruling Defence Council in Kampala.

ANGUS: Where am I?

AMOS: This is the bungalow home of Superintendent Ali Towilli. We are in Jinja which is, as you know, forty miles north-east of Entebbe.

ANGUS: Ali who?

AMOS: Superintendent Towilli is the boss-man of the State Research Bureau of Uganda. It was formerly a part of the Public Safety Unit. As I say he is not –

ANGUS: You are British?

AMOS: Yes, indeed. Very proud.

ANGUS: But acting in what capacity?

AMOS: My orders were to come here and explore the situation, direct orders from Ruling Defence Council. What you mean is – Britain HMG has no direct diplomatic link with Uganda but the Government House office keeps three secretaries at the French Consulate –

ANGUS: Then let me speak to the French Consul!

AMOS: I think you ought to know that President the Field Marshal Amin has already given audience to M. Pierre Renard, from the French Consulate, and M. Renard recommended me to see you first. Although I have no direct link with HMG

I am free to pass on all matters British as it were to the highest level in Kampala. Now . . . if you'll bear with me . . . [*From the documents*.] . . . Your name is –

ANGUS: Greville William Allnutt.

AMOS: Your name is . . . eh – Angus Fraser.

ANGUS: The name is Greville William Allnutt.

AMOS: Eh – Dr Angus Fraser.

ANGUS: I am referred to as a doctor. Indeed, I use it deliberately, in my business practice. As Dr G. W. Allnutt.

AMOS: I see.

ANGUS: Clearly, there has been some monumental blunder.

AMOS: You say you are not Dr Angus Fraser?

ANGUS: Allnutt is the name. A patronymic which, along with equally ancient designations as Clutterbuck, Bigglesthwaite or anything ending with Stein, seems to produce a wave of adolescent humour on a level not unadjacent to lavatory graffiti . . .

AMOS: Nevertheless, you are a 'doctor'?

ANGUS: When I left U K to work in Tanzania three years ago, I was a qualified veterinary surgeon. In due course, by a series of good luck and blind judgement, I accepted a government post analysing cattle vaccines, specializing in certain areas of immunology, and the title stuck. It added a useful bonus to my salary.

AMOS: And eh . . . you insist you are not Dr Angus Fraser?

ANGUS: I do not know such a name, I have never assumed such a name, and you will see from my passport, I see it is there before – indeed I am G. W. of the funny-haha surname.

AMOS: Ah . . . umm, quite.

ANGUS: On a fairly run-of-the-mill passport bearing Her Britannic Majesty's reasonable request that I may be allowed to pass freely without let or hindrance, even, dare I mention it, be afforded such assistance and protection as maybe necessary wherever I might find myself.

AMOS: The ambiguities have not escaped me, sir.

ANGUS: I have been locked up downstairs, in what I can only take for a concreted pig-bunker, for two nights, without light or food, and briefly I was allowed a drink half an hour before they brought me up to you.

AMOS: Yes well . . . for pretty brutal but obvious reasons, they don't have many actual cells in this part of town. Principally, simple truth is they don't waste much time with any bod they pick up v. quick goodnight Irene and a bathe in the river Kioga. You seem pretty certain I must say . . .

ANGUS: About what?

AMOS: Certain you are not Angus Fraser.

ANGUS: Greville is the name. I am married to a nice lady born in the Potteries, born Alice Chandley, mother of two boys of mine, George and Edward, and for eight years we lived happily in number 4, Edgemount Close, Hereford.

AMOS: And you insist you are as it says here you are – one G. W.–

AMOS: ⎱
ANGUS: ⎰ – Allnutt.

ANGUS: My mother's maiden name Tuppersley, she and my father William, were married 14 December 1927, Church of All Souls, Parish of Shrub End, Worcestershire Diocese, and, sad as I am the passport does not include these details, I won a Deacon Andrews Scholarship to Lucton Preparatory School at the age of ten.

AMOS: But you are a doctor?

ANGUS: Later, in my advanced teens, I failed to gain a selection for the science Tripos at St David's University, Lampeter, and I enrolled with desperation in an advanced students' course of animal surgery at Burford, Oxon; a venture jointly financed by the late great Lord Nuffield and a dog biscuit manufacturer who had retired to Cap Grasse on the French Med.

AMOS: All to the good . . . old fellow . . . I must soldier through all this nevertheless. You have no address in London?

ANGUS: My wife and I share a stucco white cement rendered flat-roofed community apartment by the sea, north of Dar-es-Salaam, at Tanga, built by the Chinese ten years ago for workers on the state iron-ore smelting plant. I live between this said plant and a palm oil refinery, at a humble address, titled P.O. Box 900, Avenue Chou en-Lai, and I last visited London to see Danny Kaye at the London Palladium in 1951.

AMOS: You have never been a First Secretary to the Foreign and Commonwealth Office?

ANGUS: No I have never had such a posting.

AMOS: Never worked as direct liaison with the East African Advisory Board?

ANGUS: True.

AMOS: With direct responsibility to the office of the Assistant Under-Secretary of State – ? Commonwealth Office?

ANGUS: Absolutely.

AMOS: You . . . eh . . . have lived in Nairobi a number of years –

ANGUS: I have not.

AMOS: Your wife has maintained a teaching post there –

ANGUS: She has not.

AMOS: All in all, you insist you are who you say you are, and anything said to the contrary is false?

ANGUS: I'm glad you have come round to seeing it my way.

AMOS: Well, sir, I have to tell you that this makes it very difficult for all parties concerned.

ANGUS: It does, does it? Why?

AMOS: If all this information I have here can be firmly disproved, things might go more smoothly; but you have no idea of the detail and surveillance every UK citizen is undergoing at this time in this country. Why . . . were you seen loitering outside Entebbe airport three days ago?

ANGUS: I was flying East African Airlines from Lusaka, where I had attended a conference of animal-feed bacteriologists, with particular concern for new enzootics created by grain cargo deficiencies. I had planned to stop off at Entebbe to meet friends. If I did not find them at the airport, they'd leave a car for me to pick up. No soon as I landed, I was told the crew had been arrested, reasons not stated.

AMOS: You were seen driving a green BMW with Uganda nameplates six hours after passing through customs.

ANGUS: I have friends at Jinja. Naomi and Karl Murchison. Karl is a Dutch Reform Church missionary based here. His wife told me to find the car keys under the off-side wheel hub outside the airport where Karl had left them, and drive out she said to Jinja. When I arrived at the mission house, I was told that Mrs Murchison had been taken away. And that I must wait for her. The boy did not stop to talk. He ran off.

AMOS: You were not aware of the banning of all cars for the time being?

ANGUS: Maybe I was – but I had no choice – what other way was there for me to get to Jinja? Walk forty miles at night with a suitcase?

AMOS: Mrs Murchison has not been located anywhere. There is no evidence that she even spoke to you. Nor is there any boy from the mission house.

ANGUS: The boy was Catholic Bantu, I think called – Bumali.

AMOS: Why were you staying at this empty mission house when you were picked up by officers of the State Research Bureau?

ANGUS: I was silly enough to wait around to see if either Naomi or Karl might return. Or the boy. Nobody did. I then took it into my own hands to drive the BMW back to the airport hoping the plane would take me on to Dar. That is, if it was still there. I had no means of getting in touch with anyone – the phone mysteriously packed up – nobody arrived – and these hoodlums in khaki stopped me. At gun-point. Took away all cash I had on me. Emptied the car of petrol. And drove me pillion motorbike to here at night.

AMOS: Back to Jinja.

ANGUS: And I know nothing more. It is a simple story. And I wish only for a telephone which works that I might speak to my wife and boys, explain where I am, and, hopefully provide myself with the wherewithal to get out of here, whatever it takes.

AMOS: I am afraid I am also requested to ask you what properties you own freehold or otherwise in Uganda?

ANGUS: None.

AMOS: Have you ... ever ... conspired to assassinate the President of Uganda?

ANGUS: No I have not.

AMOS: Have you ever met with or conversed with any Asians you may know, no matter how brief the connection, who themselves have shown keenness to assassinate the President of Uganda?

ANGUS: No.

AMOS: I have a . . . further . . . item . . . here; yes – on Thursday morning last you were seen talking to an Asian, on a street corner, beside the Chrysler-Africa billboard? Jinja south, Gadaphi Market Place. You handed him certain papers?

ANGUS: I have no recollection.

AMOS: There is indisputable evidence for this.

ANGUS: I just don't give a wild damn if the United Nations saw it, it means nothing to me. Nor should it to you, whoever you are.

[AMOS *stands.*]

AMOS: This meeting is closed. I'll take you back to the cell. I will get back to you as soon as I can.

ANGUS: Is that all? All you've got to say!

AMOS: Old man, thank your stars – at least you've got me.

[*The light changes.*
At the back of a hangar-like wall stands a Bell 600 helicopter.
IDI *sits inside the glass dome. The crackle from a transmitter stabs the air. It is his own voice on Radio Uganda.*
AMOS *smartly approaches and taps on the glass wing door.* IDI *gestures for him to sit beside him.*]

AMOS: . . . Mr President, sir?

IDI: Come and sit down . . . Command Post full of howling wives talking about Swiss Bank Accounts and numbered vault boxes . . . I tell them I haven't any and I tell you the truth and not one of them believes me. Women! They have been reading French magazines, always think the President of this or that has got a box of gold. I'm no common thief from my own land. What box of gold?

AMOS: Very fine machine this, Mr President.

IDI: That's right. I got sixty-five Bell 600 copters and no gasoline to fly them with, even if I had gasoline I couldn't trust four Russian-trained pilots to switch on the windscreen wipers, let alone take it up.

AMOS: Unusual ... eh ... place to meet in at your request, of course, sir.

IDI: What's the use ... no use meeting in the Security Council Room, or at the Command Post, I've locked the cabinet up in the Command Post and I've told the entire chiefs of staff to stay in that cabinet room until they devise a system of government which stops spreading thousands of leaflets demanding my resignation and other actions of public revolt against me, in person me, because as I tell them, they are doing exactly what those revisionist Zionist western capitalists want. Play into their hands. Put back Africa, black Africa hundred years my resignation would.

AMOS: Yes sir.

[*This new* IDI *is a quiet figure. Softly spoken and heavy and there is a certain sadness. A clumsy egg walking toe tongue quality. The rambler of the dream is quite different from this heavy and ponderous man.*]

IDI: All history books tell the story of millions of blacks in Africa, untold in their numbers, century after century, blacks burned, blacks hung, blacks genocide, black slaver-ships, black sweated labour, half the gold half the diamonds, half the iron-ore entire black continent ripped off and they white hypocrites in London or Paris say to me, 'Big bad black boy, you killed couple of thousand dissidents, you are worse than Hitler.'

AMOS: With respect, sir – I have interviewed the Britisher from the plane. The doctor.

IDI: He's a spy.

AMOS: Difficult to pin it on him.

IDI: Can be done.

AMOS: Legally, lawfully, that is, sir.

IDI: He's a British doctor. Secret spy from Commonwealth Office. He is Angus Fraser.

AMOS: Sir, he claims to be Greville William Allnutt.

IDI: No. I know he is Fraser.

AMOS: I am in the dark here – sir – who is this Fraser?

IDI: He says he is a secretary, East African Advisory Board, Commonwealth Office, London. But he is not.

AMOS: Who then is he?

IDI: He is this man you have here in the disguise of the other one.

AMOS: Other one?

IDI: Fraser one.

AMOS: I don't see the connecting link as it were, why should Fraser want to be Allnutt or Allnutt pretend not to be Fraser?

IDI: And this other one – this Indian – you've seen him?

AMOS: He is being brought in, sir.

IDI: He has to be brought in alive.

AMOS: I have heard nothing to the contrary.

IDI: The other one, the Asian Indian one, is called Baru – Sindi Baru.

AMOS: Quite.

IDI: It doesn't matter what name he says he is, he is Baru. And he has been seen talking to the other one the British one.

AMOS: And the one knows the other, sir, is that it?

IDI: Years ago, after we changed King's African Rifles to Uganda Rifles, and Iain Grahame. You remember Iain, Major?

AMOS: I remember Iain Grahame well, sir. Last I heard of him he was on British television putting up a spirited defence on your behalf to the British public at large.

IDI: Iain came from Sandhurst.

AMOS: Best training ground for future men on earth, sir.

IDI: My son my son . . . Gamal . . . Gamal Abdal – Nazzar Ja-Wami I wanted to please the British give them something to look up to and send the boy there but first he is a Muslim and that is not Sandhurst.

AMOS: Now . . . sir . . . about these two men – with the separate names –

IDI: Years ago after King's African Rifles became Uganda Rifles, I was told by Prophet John, told me when I would die and who would be the killer and I never did believe him I told him the old fool he was. Until I ... had this dream.

AMOS: Dream, sir – ?

IDI: No. Dreams. They are many now. They come back and it is the same names – these Britishers and Asian there, same names, talking about compensation for Asians who bled my country white, and then the dreams do not go away. I see this man who kills me. And his accomplice. Beside you, there, too.

AMOS: I assuredly pray I do not appear beside them sir –

IDI: You in the dream.

AMOS: Oh no sir, not me, sir.

IDI: But I forgive you for that. I know my Amos like I know Baruch-Bar-Lev, in Israel. I trust rank and honesty. And I like what you are for me. You are British Great British Amos Queen's British as it was when we had old Baganda days. Now ... British race of washing-machine rats. Receiver of western dumping little island. England become everybody's roast pig on a spit because everyone know the proud note is all the international strength the island got. British people think they have no censorship entire press stained with secrecy no one wants to tell the British public that gold now become totally devalued because Portugal, only country left with vast gold and no international debts wants to sell it over the counter, little Britishers with fat sums invested in South Africa aren't told that. Suddenly the Queen's sceptre not worth the nickel. In the street western capitalist nations still dreaming diamonds and gold future contain nothing like that at all bourgeois rubbish future contain continent of Africa rich and black future contain continent of South America Marxist and rich nothing else inbetween but decay and rot and do you know how many Scots landowners own the entire length of the River Tweed great River Tweed through Berwickshire – ?

AMOS: No, sir, I don't.

IDI: My information is – twenty-two.

AMOS: Absolutely shocking piece of information, sir.

IDI: Now I have had this dream again ... and they kill me. Now, they the British are hunting me down. Those whom I have given the most favours to. Factories, employment, friendship against the advice of all my Sudan and Libyan friends – you go back to those men – you find their real names – I don't want to put those Mafuta Mingi men put on them. I don't want them degooded. Don't want them treated like common *magendo* trash, but you find out where their friends, and what guns they got, who is financing this? Remember Amos you, too, were in these dreams. But you had nothing to do with it, you are a Sandhurst man. I will tell you by phone where and when to meet. I must have the truth out of them.

[AMOS *climbs out from the Bell and smartly salutes.*]

AMOS: Sir!

Jinja bungalow of TOWILLI'S.

[*This time there is debris and chaos from a ransacking job. Everything is strewn.* MAJOR AMOS *tries to clear the floor for a chair. The desk is upturned.*

Above his head the electric fan has stopped. AMOS *pauses amidst the chaos. The tiredness of the day.* AMOS *takes out a coloured neckerchief from his pocket. He wipes the perspiration from the back of his collar. He appears to have stood there waiting for a long time, but it has all been seconds.*

Banging and shoving and a half-naked 'SINDI' *is brought through the door. He is chained. There is blood and contusion on him:* AMOS *barely looks up.*

'SINDI' *stands shocked. Waiting for the door to slam behind him. During this scene a flashlight bright as a lighthouse reflector bursts through the window-panes. It sidles backwards and is then switched off.*]

AMOS: Right . . . according to my instructions we will have little trouble with you. You have good English?

SINDI: Oh yes, sir, Major sir.

AMOS: Report says you have good command of Somali, and a smatter of Nubian West Nile dialect?

SINDI: Yes sir, I do.

AMOS: How come?

SINDI: I work for Jallaquar, one-arm bandit East African

concession, Kenya, Sudan, Uganda, Tanzania, Zambia. All fruit machine collection and gift trade is authorized through the company's official carrier. I have been a senior carrier with Jallaquar since 1968.

AMOS: Oh, yes.

SINDI: I understand I was arrested and brought here on a case of mistaken identity nothing about which I know at all.

AMOS: You were picked up by the State Research Bureau on the strict authority of the Superintendent Towilli, Ali Towilli.

SINDI: I have not spoken with Towilli.

AMOS: At this stage of events, nor have I. I believe Towilli himself has been put into detention in the Nile Hotel under suspicion of mutiny. And he is the head of police as you might say.

SINDI: I don't see how I can be detained then, if –

AMOS: Look, laddie – the whole point of this matter is not to detain you, it is to let you go free. You were interrogated at four a.m. this morning by senior members of the Kampala Command Post HQ?

SINDI: I was informally introduced to six Arab gentlemen, who claimed they were personal staff to the President. They made their presence felt in various parts of my anatomy. Since then I have been sick, frequently, coughed blood, and lost all feeling in my right arm. My ears maintain a peculiar feeling also.

AMOS: Appears to have a certain humorous approach.

SINDI: I know Uganda and love it well, and the people here; what has happened to me is not so very different from hundreds of others accidentally caught up in this situation, I particularly refer to Kenyans caught on or near the border; and arbitrarily dealt with in the most vicious manner. Fortunately for myself, I do carry all correct papers of identification, my British passport and my Sudanese citizenship.

AMOS: Everything tidy and neatly in place . . . an answer for almost everything . . . what are you a Paki?

SINDI: I am a Baluchi Muslim. My parents were killed in the massacres after partition in 1948, when the Muslim League could not support those in the north-west against the merciless Hindu onslaught. In fact, what Urdu I could speak then I have utterly put aside. I am British and Sudanese, above all I am Muslim.

AMOS: Highly articulate ... born Pakistan ... professes Muslim faith or ideology. Parents killed by Hindu nationalists after UK get out. Right you are!

[*Searchlight flicks across windows. A rotation from its regularity it would appear.*]

SINDI: Why are we being flashed like this ... ?

AMOS: Sonny ... that I cannot give an exact reply to ... it may be, as this is the house of the police superintendent, and as he himself is under lock and key, there must be those factions who consider anyone caught inside the building highly suspect. Including me. Are you aware of the situation out there in the streets? No petrol. Little electricity. Food down to bananas and Red Cross stores' dried milk, and every office and bank in Kampala is closed. All four borders to the country are blocked. And you ask me about flashing lights! I don't wish to unnerve your tough little Paki shell but this is a state of chronic emergency.

SINDI: I do not understand who I am speaking to; if you might be so kind as to enlighten me?

AMOS: I am a mere liaison officer between all British passport holders in Uganda and the *pro tem.* UK Office in the French Consulate. It is my sad duty to keep any one – Britons or blue passport wogs carrying this – [*Holds up the passport.*] like yourself the hell out of this country because it is *pro tem.* and very *tem.* at that about to allow the shit to hit the fan at the highest diplomatic level. Now ... just what were you doing driving that motorbike through the Kenya border up towards Jinja?

SINDI: I was lost. There was not a single light at night. All road signs had been smashed down.

AMOS: Where were you intended for?

SINDI: I had an appointment with a spare parts retailer, German-based firm of Schweikers Son Ltd, at Busia, but all road signs were down. I then decided to head on inland when I knew from Southern Cross star light that Jinja lay west at the angle of ninety degrees, and I had a fruit machine plastic component assembly gentleman to see, who had offered high-margin deductions if we considered his apparatus. In fact, it would seem, his type of plastic has an asbestos base which allows for considerable strength –

AMOS: In all this, you had no idea or thought that the entire country might lie on the verge of flames?

SINDI: Sir, with respect, I am a business agent, and my work takes me through six or seven East African countries, revolutions and uprisings need not interfere with the commercial progress.

AMOS: You say so?

SINDI: With the greatest respect, sir, I do, sir.

[AMOS *leans over his papers on the desk and writes wearily.*]

AMOS: Full name?

SINDI: Isaid Dem Ala-Messid Jalli.

AMOS: Nationality?

SINDI: Sudanese joint UK citizenship.

AMOS: Place of birth?

SINDI: Shikapur, Baluchistan; West Pakistan.

AMOS: Present occupation?

SINDI: ... Sales carrier for East African Fruit Machine concessions.

AMOS: Now ... Laddie ... this is not the information I was led to believe you had handed over freely and voluntarily back in your cell this morning?

SINDI: No, sir.

AMOS: I'd like you to remind me, what facts you gave freely and voluntarily, to these men?

SINDI: I had as sensible a conversation as I could with them, and they duly informed me of their position. If I did not comply freely and voluntarily, I would be 'finished off slowly' I think are the exact words.

AMOS: Well ... for your benefit ... I'll outline what this refers. They mean, dear lad, they take you to a quiet patch of ground, and cut off your private pieces, these, along with your tongue which by then you have also parted company with are stuffed down your throat. Limb by limb you are severed into portions. If you live long enough, you are encouraged to eat portions of this broken-up anatomy.

SINDI: I see.

AMOS: Believe you me, it is a form of persuasion these men are very accustomed to.

SINDI: Quite.

AMOS: Meanwhile, they did make it clear to you, just what exactly they wanted you to tell them?

SINDI: Perfectly.

AMOS: And you have memorized all this?

SINDI: To the very best of my ability.

AMOS: Right then . . . shall we try again?

[*He pulls out a further length of notepaper. He draws the typewriter close to his chest and awkwardly fingers the keys.*]

Your full name is –

SINDI: Sindi Baru.

AMOS: Nationality?

SINDI: UK passport holder resident in Sudan.

AMOS: Your origin of birth?

SINDI: I was born in Staling Grove, Wolverhamptonshire.

AMOS: Wolverhampton.

SINDI: Woverhamptonshire.

AMOS: No shire . . .

SINDI: I apologize.

AMOS: Present occupation?

SINDI: Spokesman and principal advocate, acting-chairman of the Society for Disenfranchised Asian Peoples –

AMOS: Communities.

SINDI: Society for Disenfranchised Asian Communities. If I may say so, sir – 'peoples' seems a much more democratic word than 'communities' with all its echoes of sectarian groupings.

AMOS: You could be right. Now – you are aware that this

Society is banned in Uganda, and any propaganda affiliated hereto is also banned?

SINDI: I am.

AMOS: In addition – there is concern in Uganda about those who finance this Society. You are prepared freely and voluntarily to declare their names.

SINDI: It is a mixture of the CIA and various Zionist fronts from London and Paris, notably Marks and Spencers Ltd, Safeways and Pricerite stores, Tesco Trading Company and the Rothschild Banque Centrale, Avenue Marceaux, Paris huitième.

AMOS: You immediately made contact once you arrived at Jinja, without having passed any normal Ugandan border posts, made contact with whom?

SINDI: An Englishman.

AMOS: His name?

SINDI: Angus Fraser.

AMOS: Where was this?

SINDI: Beneath the Chrysler-Africa billboard, Jinja south, Gadaphi Market Square.

AMOS: What was the point of this meeting?

SINDI: To ascertain just how much danger the remaining Ugandan Asians face if the President were to be assassinated by an Indian.

AMOS: By you, you mean.

SINDI: I discussed this point with my six interrogators from Command Post HQ, Kampala; and I persuaded them I do not know one end of a gun from the other. I was not prepared to go any further than this. I was not prepared to commit suicide. My name is now Sindi Baru, and my concern is for the safety of all Asians left in this country on behalf of this Society for Disenfranchised Asian Communities.

AMOS: Are you prepared to sign this document?

SINDI: It is on the understanding that I am not the fish the authorities are interested in – it is the Britisher, this man called Fraser.

AMOS: Correct.

SINDI: And furthermore, on the understanding that I will be immediately released, and allowed to leave the country.

AMOS: Almost correct.

SINDI: A hitch? Sir, do I hear?

AMOS: I am to give you clothes, and set you free once you have signed this document. There is no risk from anyone in this bungalow because I think you will discover the place is now empty but for you and me. Will you sign please?

[AMOS *pauses to watch* 'SINDI' *sign the document he pulls out from the typewriter. There is a duplicate.*]

SINDI [*glancing up*]: ... This ... Sindi Baru ... seems a remarkably silly person, if I may say so, someone who doesn't seem to know how to keep out of trouble?

[AMOS *collects both signed documents. He pulls out from a bag some loose clothing. Slacks and vest and sandals.* 'SINDI' *hastily slips in to them.*]

AMOS: My advice is ... as quickly as you can get to the border. Wait until night. Walk in the coolness. You might make it to Jaluo in twenty hours. Avoid all lorries. Don't accept lifts. Trust no one.

SINDI: My papers please?

AMOS: Ahh ... I think you will find, Mr Baru, it will be safer without any documentation whatsoever.

[AMOS *takes the passport, which is in the name of its rightful owner,* ISAID DEM ALA-MESSID JALLI, *and places it in a transparent zip-folder. He puts the folder in his inside pocket.* 'SINDI' *stares with dismay at* AMOS. *By* AMOS' *side the telephone commences to ring.* AMOS *reaches for it slowly.* 'SINDI' *hurriedly makes for the door.*]

A door to a cell.

[*Bars.* 'ANGUS FRASER' *looking weak and tired is drawn towards the grill in the door. Single naked bulb.*]

VOICE: Dr Allnutt?

ANGUS: Is that you, Major?

VOICE: Never you mind who it is.

ANGUS: I would like the use of a telephone.

VOICE: Out of the question. I'm afraid there is only one public utility line working and you wouldn't like that one.

ANGUS: I want to see a representative from the French Consulate.

VOICE: That has already been put into action. Someone will come to you.

ANGUS: I'm hungry.

VOICE: When did you last eat?

ANGUS: I think perhaps two nights back. The time does strange things –

VOICE: Have you water?

ANGUS: I use the water kept in the disposal bucket. I put earth over my waste material.

VOICE: Perfectly sensible.

ANGUS: I didn't think I'd be grateful for an earth floor. How long will I be here?

VOICE: I do not know.

ANGUS: Is there any way that London or even a colleague can be informed?

VOICE: London is *au fait*.

ANGUS: Can they do anything?

VOICE: I'm afraid no.

ANGUS: I've . . . got a lady wife . . . and two boys . . . that I'd love . . . love to meet again.

VOICE: Steady . . . steady? . . .

ANGUS: Y . . . yes . . .

VOICE: Hang in there, what?

ANGUS: Not very apt recommendation this precise moment.

VOICE: Sorry about that . . . now – have you spoken to anyone?

ANGUS: No.

VOICE: No peculiar happenings?

ANGUS: Sometimes I hear firing . . . now and then the light bulb dies on me . . . I have for company what appears to be a five-legged rat who has two other chums, and when I wake up the lice tend to shelter in my nostrils although I have expressly forbidden this on account that any gathering of three

persons or more shall be deemed a public meeting and carries
a death penalty.

VOICE: Nobody has coerced you into signing anything?

ANGUS: Nothing.

VOICE: Right you are.

ANGUS: What will become of me?

VOICE: Touch wood old chap.

ANGUS: I tend to eat it rather than – present diet conditions.

VOICE: One final question, old boy – are you or have you ever
been known as Angus Fraser or Dr Angus Fraser?

ANGUS: Never.

VOICE: Can you assure me of that? On oath?

ANGUS: There are only about three things worth making an
oath upon – the Holy Bible, the Union Jack or one's mother.
I don't possess the former, as for the latter two, they are both
dead anyway. Would my life insurance do instead?

VOICE: That's it – keep up the chin.

ANGUS [*softly*]: Help me . . . you bastard . . .

 [*Silence.*]

 . . . Major!

[*Lights change to the far corner where* 'SINDI' (ISAID *in
reality*) *is walking across country at night. Occasionally truck
lights flash past him. He blinks and walks on bloody and
dishevelled.*]

[*The lights lift on a vast bare area.
More like a hangar but it is a disused passenger lounge at
Entebbe. Filthy white walls. Litter and graffiti. Stars of
David. Shaloms. Bullet holes everywhere. Broken glass
upper-panes. Steel doors barred with chains. Naked lamps
swinging.
* AMOS *enters, he does not see* IDI *immediately. Sound of gunfire. Bulbs flicker low. Beneath the windows lie the unmounted
frames of a number of 106 mm nozzles. There are moments of
complete light failure during this scene.*]

AMOS: . . . Mr President, sir?

IDI: Present, Major.

AMOS: Ah . . . but there are no guards outside?

IDI: I leave these PLF fighters in the Command Post.

AMOS: But you have to have a bodyguard, sir – ?

IDI: No. Safer without.

AMOS: Sir – ?

IDI: I don't sleep well . . . men about men lying outside the door, men sitting on the window rails, I don't sleep so well. No privacy now.

AMOS: Price of fame and power, sir.

IDI: I am tired now.

AMOS: Yes sir, quite.

IDI: Better here . . . they all gone away.

AMOS: Absolutely and definitely . . . the mind needs respite . . . ease of mind . . . change the pace.

IDI: Yes, Major.

AMOS: V. refreshing, sir.

IDI: You done what I asked, Major?

AMOS: Sir!

IDI: You saw the Indian?

AMOS: Sir!

IDI: And that Britisher?

AMOS: Sir! The doctor.

IDI: I don't want Towilli's men torturing and brutalizing these men, I want to show them mercy, I want a public trial, here are these people with UK passports here I have a UK passport. Brought to a fair trial and public punishment. A Ugandan Peoples' Tribunal.

AMOS: I spoke with the Britisher, sir.

IDI: What is his name?

AMOS: Name is . . . Angus Fraser, sir. No doubt about that.

IDI: The Indian?

AMOS: Name is Sindi Baru, sir. I have filed his complete confession with the State Research Bureau. He is a dead man.

IDI: Where is he?

AMOS: I put him back sir where he was first placed, the Makindye Military Prison.

IDI: The Britisher?

AMOS: I put him in the Makindye, sir.

IDI: I'd like to speak to them . . . tell them about their bad ways
. . . but I feel sorry for them. Not their fault. Little people.
Tools of the West. British tools. Oh Britain think they rule
the waves the flag been rolled up long time gone now what
the famous English weekly the *Spectator* say of me day of
accession 30 January 1971 say – 'We cannot say we learn of
the overthrow of Dr Milton Obote of Uganda with any great
regret: if a choice is to be made between quiet military men
and noisy civil dictators then we prefer in Africa at least the
quiet military.' Say that, the English *Spectator*. Then say the
weekly *New Statesman*, *New Statesman* 29 January 1971, say –
'So far as Britain is concerned Amin will undoubtedly be
easier to deal with than the abrasive Obote!' Now . . . what
they scheming – assassination they scheme. Bring that Indian
in here to kill me. I had a dream. And I remembered his
name. Forget it is Dada Amin they deal with they who in-
vented me all those jokes clever English comics funny stories
. . . I never ride the same jeep . . . never say where I go next
. . . never tell them which wife I sleep with . . . who I eat with
. . . run . . . run . . . keep on . . . an Olympic athlete Akii Bua
would have won in Montreal if I had sent him . . . Now they
think send me an Indian he has a chance, what, Major?

AMOS: Not a chance in the world, sir.

IDI: If he got to me, he could never get out of Uganda alive. I'd
be a martyr.

AMOS: Absolutely, sir.

IDI: They know they cannot find a black boy dare try to kill me.
Nobody not even my enemies would do that. They know
what it look like just black Africa bunch of grape coons unable
to keep peace between themselves always killing each other,
funny niggers and wogs always behave like that.

AMOS: Not too many blacks would dare try, Mr President.

IDI: It is the perfect thing the British think, oh send some half-
crazed Asian got a raw deal some time in Uganda, excuse
enough get rid of him afterwards.

AMOS: Quite, sir. And I somehow don't think he would finish the job. All bunglers these bods, no army training behind, hit and miss.

IDI: What would you say, Major, if it was a white who tried assassinate Idi Amin?

AMOS: Not possible, sir.

IDI: Why not?

AMOS: No way out. Stands out a mile in this country. Certain death.

IDI: Impossible, Major?

AMOS: He'd have to lay plans mighty carefully. No border country could bail him out. He'd be entirely on his own, sir.

IDI: What he do it for, Major? The money?

AMOS: He couldn't escape.

IDI: You know who laughing if I die, Major? The right wing of the world laughing.

AMOS: Don't follow you, sir?

IDI: Little Asian get to me with a grenade or a revolver – Vorster laughing, Kissinger laughing, all these right-wing English papers laughing, Israel laughing, and France . . . But it would never be a white man. What do you say?

AMOS: Or perhaps he could lay a good false scent. Give him time to get out quite respectably.

[*The light bulbs are on the blink. Gunfire increases. Both men listen to it.*]

IDI: When I threw out those Asians, I paid Africa's debt in full. Why do you thing Banda in Malawi has ordered all Asian shopkeepers out of the rural areas? The British put them here. They can take them away.

AMOS: Sir?

IDI: This is the old passenger embarkation room, Entebbe. I let those Jews stay here while I tried to barter for their lives. Kenya and CIA and New York Zionists attack, daren't see the OAU President make big success of the various top-level discussion, no good to see a black sergeant they want to topple make a hit with Israeli passengers I like Jews only want to see Dada Amin come down because they have a separate plan, nobody in entire history ever been assassinated in a vacuum, when I am gone look round your back garden and ask who profit and point your finger. You know who I had in here? Had meet me?

AMOS: Sir?

IDI: Oh all come here meet Amin . . . Kissinger arrive . . . big red carpet. . . . Brezhnev arrive . . . Chou en-Lai . . . Whitlam . . . Gadaphi my friend . . . James Callaghan . . . West Germany man . . . French President before last . . . all come here . . . suddenly Uganda got the spotlight of the world . . . all black children look up see Big Daddy say yea I kill, yea my enemies will suffer, but this is a black African man saying too. He say children look up it will be blood at the tip of Africa, it will be Muslim and Marxist call-to-arms bring Namibia into arms of those black children what white man who can bomb Nagasaki can call a black leader a tyrant fear!

[*The lights finally dim to nothing. Blackness. Gunfire in the distance.*]

IDI's VOICE: Do you see, Major?

AMOS' VOICE: Not a thing, sir.

[*In the darkness a square of light is lit.* ALLNUTT *is lying in a cramped earth dug-out no larger than a grave hole. He is bloodied and weak, but alive.*
The image blacks.]

IDI: Before the fall of Obote, people said I knew too much about Obote's ivory. And Obote collected ivory. And people said the British must have been involved in the plot against Obote. I never denied it.

[*The lights flicker back on. The firing fades away.*]

IDI: Talk to me, Major, less of this 'sir' and that 'sir', what you saying to me Major when you sleep at night?

AMOS: What would you like to hear me say, Mr President?

IDI: Talk about the past, Major. You remember the old past? We fought together against the Mau Mau. I was a corporal in the King's African Rifles. At Tuso we killed them, at Kairo, at Kinyono, and Kangema we killed them down. Then in

Karamoja we degooded the Pokot tribe, and one whole Turkana village we provided them with a proper funeral, wasn't that so, Major?

AMOS: Sir?

IDI: It was the past wasn't it? It was there then. And I was still the sergeant. Though I was the heavyweight champion of Uganda. I think ... I still am the heavyweight champion of Uganda. As a sergeant I'd go up to the barrack Commander, Major Iain Grahame, I'd say look at these new officers you have made, sir! Lieutenant Okahura, Lieutenant Ndalebo, Lieutenant Oyite, all drunk sir, dogs lying kicking their legs up all *pombe* drunk, sir! But not me, sir, I am a Muslim.

AMOS: Absolutely.

IDI: Talk to me about the old King's African Rifles? ...

AMOS: Ah ... ehr ... Mr President remembers those happy days recruiting in Karamoja in '62. When you asked a Suk recruit to kill a snake to test his accuracy he said, oh no, he said, the soul of the dead Suk always returned into a snake. So Mr President spends the next two weeks shooting every damn snake he can see in the bush to try break the silly superstition.

IDI [*smiling warmly*]: Never broke it for good.

AMOS: Sir remembers the day whites opened up the officers' messroom to all African officers and senior men and when I walked in with you and you ordered a beer that Asian barman was so scared of serving you I had to take him by the throat and shake him like a rattlesnake tell him it's all right you silly bleeder the sergeant can be served a beer!

IDI: He ran out the door like a wildebeest!

AMOS: There was old Colonel Tom 'Diddles' Parker ... Old Parksy ... Fossbender with the white eyebrows.

IDI: Captain Henry Fossbender.

AMOS: Larry Merridew.

IDI: Lieutenant the medic always filled his syringes with water always did the trick the men never came back with another complaint!

AMOS: Marcos Rodd.

IDI: Old Mauritio ... what he do Mauritio now, he went to Fort Portal –

AMOS: They say he bought out the entire boot quota from the British for a thousand shillings, he set up shop with more boots than we could –

IDI: I tell you he had more boots than we got Ugandans in the whole of Uganda!

AMOS: That's right, sir! Jolly funny story.

IDI: You went to Sandhurst, Amos?

AMOS: Sir.

IDI: High-class English school?

AMOS: Haileybury, sir.

IDI: And you went abroad?

AMOS: Gibraltar, Hong Kong, Malaya, NATO serving in Turkey, relief-force volunteers in the Trucial States ... everywhere, sir.

IDI: Yes. And you met the Queen?

AMOS: I had the honour of an introduction once from the one-time governor of Kenya, Sir Evelyn Baring.

IDI: But you never took a wife?

AMOS: I ... keep out of trouble, sir.

IDI: What do you stay for here in Uganda?

AMOS: If sir recalls, I am now a Ugandan citizen. Long time since have I given up my home passport. There is no leaving ...

IDI: But, what do you stay for, Amos?

AMOS: Well, sir, if you had seen it the way I have. Up country, the Rift Valley, Murchison National Park, the Karamajong Hills ... the Owen Falls hydro-electric scheme ... I have stood on the shores of Lake Victoria and watched the night come down, I've watched so many purple herons, fifteen thousand or more of them, as if in separate squadrons, take an hour to flight off, to clear in the dead sun ... you'd understand ... this land is the pearl, sir.

IDI: You are the officer and the gentleman I trust.

AMOS: Sir!

IDI: All those things I say about the West don't count . . .
  Amos . . . remember it was me I was the butt sergeant.

AMOS: And I was, *pro tem.*, your Commanding Officer.

IDI [*standing*]: Firing ceased now. I think my wives ceased their
  quarrelling.

AMOS: Sir!

  [AMOS *walks away from the figure in the corner of the
  passenger lounge.*]

IDI: I go, now.

AMOS: Sir.

IDI: I go home.

  [AMOS *pauses by an unlocked door. He looks back. Takes a
  step back towards* IDI.]

AMOS: There was one more thing . . . sir . . . with respect.

  [IDI *glances up.*]

IDI: I must go.

AMOS: Mr President . . .

  [AMOS *slowly reaches for something in his pocket.*
  He draws the gun and fires.]

*Mr President, I have a message for you from a number of old
friends of yours outside Uganda –* It is a message from the
following – Brigadier Muhammed Hussein, and Colonels
M. Arach, A. Langoya, Akwango, Ojok, Abwala, Ayumi,
Ekirring, P. Obol, O. Ogwal; the soldiers and friends of
Lugbara, the men and women of Mbarra, former Prime
Minister of Uganda, Kiwanua; Vice-Chancellor of Makerere
University, Kalimuzo; Governor of the Bank of Uganda,
Mubiru; the Chief-Justice of Uganda, Benedicto Kiwanuka
and Archbishop Luwum.

  [AMOS *puts the revolver away.*
  *He takes the waterproof zip-folder from his pocket. He takes
  out Isaid's passport and tosses it on the ground beside the body.*
  AMOS *pauses.*
  *In his mind he hears a very faint echo of a military command.
  As of a parade ground command to muster.*
  AMOS *stares steadily at us. His eyeline is strangely fixed
  above our heads now. Gradually, there comes the sound of a*

military band. It is an echo in AMOS' *mind of a flag being lowered and a ceremonial strike up.*
As the music fades away, AMOS *turns and walks off.*
Comes a different sound, far away, that of the British marching out of Uganda.
Lights change.]

ACT THREE

Incidental flashback.

> [*Beneath the Chrysler-Africa billboard, Jinja south, Gadaphi Market Square. The neon blinks above the heads of the crowds. Two strangers pass by. They are* ISAID DEM ALA-MESSID JALLI *and* GREVILLE WILLIAM ALLNUTT. ISAID *sees* GREVILLE *look for a match for his cigarette.* GREVILLE *has a newspaper sticking out of his pocket.*]

GREVILLE: Ah . . . excuse me, have you a light?

ISAID: Here . . .

GREVILLE: Thank you . . .

ISAID: Is that a newspaper you have?

GREVILLE: What?

ISAID: The *Voice of Uganda* you have there?

GREVILLE: Matter of fact it's the *Times of Zambia*.

ISAID: Today's *Times*?

GREVILLE: Oh no.

ISAID: Yesterday's?

GREVILLE: Four day's old.

ISAID: I see . . . There has been no radio all day, I thought perhaps. It has been such a terrible day for me.

GREVILLE: Sorry to hear that.

ISAID: But thank you. There was nothing much of particular importance in it?

GREVILLE: No, nothing at all.

ISAID: No news, sir?

GREVILLE: Do keep it. Here.

> [GREVILLE *gives the paper to* ISAID. *They nod and go their ways amongst the crowd.*
> *Traffic and sellers and the billboard flicker.*
> *The noises diminish. Urban shadows retreat. A dust haze settles. Dusk steals light, it becomes a* kondo *evening, the stolen goods of the crepuscular. Threat of thunderous rain,*]

murmur of insect heat and corpulent frogs, borassus palm thickets . . . broken sorghum cane by the shamba *huts . . . pungent leaf mould.*]

END